Copyright 2025 Patricia Giglio
All Rights Reserved

Front cover image: Mrs. Kitchener, a female gravedigger, carries on her husband's business whilst he serves on the front, Aley Green Cemetery, Luton. Measuring the grave. (Source: Imperial War Museum) Back cover image: St. Joseph Park, Rochester, NY (Source: Patricia Giglio)

ISBN 979-8-3485-2004-5

Notice: The information in the book is true and complete to the best of my knowledge. It is offered without guarantee on the part of the author. The author disclaims all liability in connection with the use of this book.

All rights reserved. No part of this book may be reproduced or transmitted in any form whatsoever without prior written permission from the author except in the case of brief quotations embodied in critical articles and reviews.

Throughout the years, the support I have received has been incredible. My husband Steve has shown such pride in my work and pushed me to continue to follow my dream, a beacon of light and grounding. My kids, Liesl and Karl, who are no longer "kids", and give me great joy in what they have achieved. It is also dedicated to my family, though many of them have passed on. Then there are my friends; Sally, Karen and Kira who allow me to be who I am and embrace (and sometimes share) in my craziness.

Here is to the books I have written and the many more to come. I wish to raise a glass to those who inspire, motivate and support me.

A GANG OF THIEVES

Joseph Loomis, a wool draper, sailed from Essex, England to the Massachusetts Bay Colony in 1638 and settled in Boston before he moved his family to Connecticut. The family were well-respected in their communities, and served as lawyers, doctors, ministers, scientists, and teachers. Somewhere along the way, though, the family strayed off the path of righteousness when they moved to Sangerfield, near Nine Mile Swamp, a 7,000-acre swamp along the Chenango River in Oneida County. It was there that the family became known as the Loomis Gang, a nineteenth-century band of outlaws.

George Washington Loomis was the patriarch of the Oneida County branch, and he was a very well-liked and respected farmer. He was educated and popular to the point that his neighbors often sought out his advice and put great stock in his opinions. George used public reverence as a smoke screen to hide his true nature. Born in Windsor, Connecticut in 1799, his mother died when George was just five years old. When he was nineteen, he moved to Vermont with his sister. The following is an excerpt from his biography on findagrave.com. It gives insight to his life of crime which had begun when he was just a young man.

He had a fondness of horses and a predilection for collecting those that did not belong to him. He learned early that stolen horses could easily be driven to Connecticut and sold with no questions asked...In 1802 he fled Randolph, Vermont just ahead of the sheriff's posse and headed towards his sister Clarissa Loomis Preston's home in Sangerfield, Oneida County, New York with over $3,000 in gold coins in his saddlebags.

His future bride, Rhoda Mallet, was not a delicate flower in the least. She often described as the "belle of the ball" with a fiery temper, a smart woman employed as a schoolteacher. Unlike George, her penchant for mischief and lawlessness was handed down by her father Zachariah Mallet. Money trouble seemed to plague Zachariah, he accrued a mountain of debt that the sheriff was instructed to collect. Mallet had been given only two choices, either give the sheriff money to post against his debt or spend time in debtors' prison. When the sheriff called on the Mallet home, Rhoda refused to let him in. The sheriff did not give up so easily and tried to enter the residence through an open window. Rhoda met him on the other side with a shovel from the fireplace and struck the lawman in the head with it. It was said that Rhoda's actions that day was the reason George wanted to take her for his bride, he said "A girl who will fight for father will fight for husband. I am going to marry that girl." Whether this part of the story is true or just part of the yarns spun in the Loomis legend is unknown. As for Rhoda's father, his money woes continued, and the sheriff seized the Mallet property in the name of Oneida County when he failed to pay his taxes and was sent to prison on the charge of perjury.

Rhoda Marie Mallet Loomis

After George and Rhoda were united in marriage, they made their home near Nine Mile Swamp and Rhoda gave him ten children, four daughters; Calista, Charlotte, Cornelia, and Lucia, as well as six sons; (in order of birth) William, Washington, Grove, Wheeler, Amos, and Hiram. As the children grew up, Rhoda made sure that they were well educated and cultured. She also took great care in teaching them the intricacies of the criminal mind. There were accounts of "Mother Loomis" telling her children that "you may steal, but if you are caught, you shall be whipped" or "don't come back without stealing something, if it's nothing but a jackknife." All the sons took up a life of crime and intimidation, but Washington was a carbon copy of his father, a charmer and a conniver. The following is an excerpt from the *History of the Loomis Gang (1877)* by Amos Cummings about Washington W. Loomis.

He was a keen observer of human nature, and seemed endowed with magnetic power. Few could resist the fascination of his manner and conversation. Detective Wilkins says that in ten minutes he could turn an enemy into a friend. He was a born diplomatist and never resorted to physical force when his ends could be obtained in any other way."

As for their daughters, three would marry into respectable families, Cornelia remained at Rhoda's side until her death.

The stories of the Loomis family's crimes and escapades are numerous, beginning when the children were young. Around 1820 a traveling peddler went missing and the last place he was known to have been was the Loomis farm. The sheriff questioned George and Rhoda, and even though he did not have a search warrant, the family allowed him to have a look around. As the sheriff became suspicious about the well that he found filled with stones. Along with his men, the sheriff began to pull the stones out of the shaft, certain that the peddler's corpse was at the bottom. Halfway down they encountered a boulder that was too large to move and that was the end of the search. It appeared that great lengths had been taken to conceal a secret. The peddler was never found. Could the Loomis family have gotten away with murder? That is an answer that will forever lie at the bottom of the well.

The older the boys got, the more involved they became in the family "business." They became good at livestock and horse theft. But they in no way limited themselves to just that. They burglarized homes and businesses, then sold the spoils to unsuspecting neighbors and even back to their victims. They also passed counterfeit bills, which was a crime that George was all too familiar with and almost landed him in prison. Counterfeiting was a blight on the country, the fake money flooded the banks and marketplaces. It was believed that the Loomis farm was a meeting place for counterfeiters. George got caught red-handed with a fake $100 bill but was able to buy his way out of the charge, while his accomplices were sent to prison.

As it was said earlier, "Mother Loomis" raised her children to be smart criminals. The Loomis boys never stole from anyone who lived near them, and they did not keep stolen property at the farm even though the 1825 homestead was built with double-paneled walls and false floors. They hid everything in the dense swamp because few, other than the boys, could navigate through it.

In the beginning, the neighbors never suspected the Loomis family of the thefts. In fact, in many instances the boys joined the posse that set out to look for the thieves. With the stolen goods hidden in the swamp, the crimes could not be linked to the Loomis family. Those who suspected the Loomis family of a crime or spoke out against them were met with swift retribution. If they talked to authorities, their house or barn would mysteriously be burned to the ground, and of course the Loomis men would undoubtably have an airtight alibi. If by chance an arrest warrant was obtained for one of the men, the charges were quickly dropped – a generous bribe paid to a judge or lost evidence made prosecution impossible.

In 1849, the sheriff got a search warrant, and a posse raided the Loomis farm. The boys were sloppy with this last heist and broke two of their cardinal rules...they stole from a neighbor and did not hide the stolen good in the swamp. The posse found twelve wagons full of their ill-gotten gains and even though the Loomis boys were basically caught with "their hand in the cookie jar," the charges brought against them did not stick. For Washington Loomis, it was too close of a call and thought it would be a good idea to leave town for a while and head west to the golden fields of California. Washington's brains and charm made him the head of the Loomis gang and his departure was a blow to the family operation. An even bigger blow was felt when their patriarch died on February 26, 1851. With both Washington and George gone, there was no one to guide the rest of the family and they took a break from the life of crime.

Washington's luck ran out in California just as it almost had in Sangerfield, and he came back to the open arms of his family. With his return, the gang was back on business and picked up right where they left off, just as if Washington had never left. At this time, the country had been thrust into a great Civil War. The Union Army needed fresh horses, and the Loomis gang knew how to get their hands on some. They stole horses from nearby farm and sold them to the US government. All the able-bodied men had enlisted and fought battles in far-off places, which led to a shortage of lawmen. This gave the Loomis gang free reign, and they became the largest family crime syndicate in America. By no means did this mean that a blind eye was turned. An indictment against the Loomis family was secured on October 10, 1864, and sat on a desk in the Oneida County courthouse until the case was to be heard. That night the courthouse burned to the ground, supposedly by Washington Loomis. This symbolic thumb to the nose toward authority would be the beginning of the end for the Loomis gang, soon it would all come crashing down around them.

At the end of the Civil War, the men who fought a bigger enemy returned home and refused to bow down to the Loomis family anymore. Those associated with the gang were picked off one by one and brutally attacked. Soon there was no one left but the Loomis boys. In the dark of night on October 29, 1865, the Sangerfield Vigilante Committee which was a group of angry men led by a local constable descended on the Loomis farm. They knocked on the door and called Washington to come outside where he was ambushed. His body was later found behind the woodshed with his skull bashed in. The vigilantes also attacked Grove. He was beaten, covered in a burlap sack soaked in kerosene and set on fire. As Cornelia beat out the flames that engulfed her brother, outside the barn burst into a raging inferno. Within a span of two hours the Loomis family's forty-five-year reign of terror ended abruptly. A year later the house was burned to the ground.

All the Loomis boys, except for Hiram, scattered across the country. Rhoda lost what was left of the farm and she, Cornelia and Hiram moved to Hastings, seventy miles north of Syracuse.

The old Loomis homestead is a few yards off the corner of Swamp and Loomis Roads in Waterville. All that remains is the foundation of the barn. The legacy of the Loomis family now lives in legends told by the campfire.

A MURDER OF CROWS IN PRISON CITY

Gathering at dusk, crows land in a tree, then scuffle and squawk...filtering down through the branches. Crows stream overhead in the later afternoon – rivers of crows. These are crows of purpose.
                                                            -Ellen Blackstone

One of the greatest phenomena in the animal kingdom is the murder of crows, as many as 20,000 to 40,000 crows traveling in one communal group. During the day they disperse across the countryside to eat, only meeting at staging areas throughout the day before they roost as dusk falls. Cemeteries are perfect roosts because they are open and have a plentiful food source. According to scientific research, a roost is used for several years before the crows move on. Auburn's Fort Hill Cemetery has been a roost for thousands of crows for decades, much to the confusion of scientists. Why do they keep returning year after year? Many believe that it has spiritual meanings connected to the deep Native American roots surrounding the cemetery.

City of Crows by alaskaraven

The site of Fort Hill Cemetery is one of the highest points in Auburn and its history goes back almost one thousand years. Within the confines of Fort Hill is the Osco Temple, a prehistoric Indian mound with dates to around 1100 AD. The temple was an ancient, fortified village used by the Cayuga Indians to protect against opposing tribes during times of war. The Cayuga used it until the early 18th century when the Iroquois Confederacy was formed, and the Cayuga were forced to find a new home. For six hundred years a patch of land near the summit was used to bury their dead. When the Cayuga left, the remains of their ancestors stayed.

The Native American connection to Auburn went farther than the Cayuga. One of the most notable Native American that called Auburn home was the son of Chief Shikellamy, John Logan, also known as John the Orator. When war and disease threatened the Cayuga, along with the Seneca and Lenape tribes, they pushed west into Ohio and formed the Mingo Tribe. Logan, like his father, believed that a friendly relationship with the settlers needed to be maintained. Everyone seemed to live in relative peace until the Yellow Creek Massacre in April 1774 during which the "Virginia Long Knives," British colonists from Virginia, killed several Mingo, including Logan's brother. Although the tribal chiefs called for a peaceful resolution, Native American tradition called for retaliation. Raids by war parties sparked Dunmore's War. The only major battle during the war did not end in the favor of the Mingo, and they were forced into a peace treaty. Logan refused to attend the treaty negotiations, and instead gave his famous speech known as Logan's Lament... *"I appeal to any white man to say if ever he entered Logan's cabin hungry, and he gave him not meat; if ever he came cold and naked, and he clothed him not. During the course of the last long and bloody war, Logan remained idle in his cabin, an advocate for peace. Such was my love for the whites, that my countrymen pointed as they passed, and said, "Logan is the friend of white men." I had even thought to have lived with you, but for the injuries of one man. Col. Cresap, the last Spring, in cold blood, and unprovoked, murdered all the relations of Logan, not sparing even my women and children. There runs not a drop of my blood in the veins of any living creature. This called on me for revenge. I have sought it: I have killed many: I have fully glutted my vengeance. For my country, I rejoice at the beams of peace. But do not harbor a thought that mine is the joy of fear. Logan never felt fear. He will not turn on his heel to save his life. Who is there to mourn for Logan? Not one.*" After giving his speech, Logan was not heard from again. His death came at the hands of his nephew in 1780 near Detroit, Michigan. There is a fifty-six-foot-tall obelisk at Fort Hill Cemetery dedicated to John Logan, it is inscribed with the last line of his lament... "Who is there to mourn for Logan."

As for the crows, they have links to Spiritualism and Native American culture. Birds, in general, are believed to carry messages between the earth and sky. Crows were seen as symbols of wisdom, perhaps the wisest of all living creatures, as well as symbols of war. Mason Winfield said it best in his book *Iroquois Supernatural*;

"*Battlefield birds are everywhere associated with war and destiny. They know where death is soon to be found and where the bodies are to be had. In their visits with the eternal, they inquire the fates of heroes. They know the ends of empires.*"

Perhaps the crows are the guardians of the Osco Temple and the Cayuga ancestors that are buried there. Or maybe the crows are the ones that mourn for Logan.

A REBEL FOR THE CAUSE

The American Civil War may have divided the country; North vs. South and brother vs. brother, but when it came to love, the Mason-Dixon Line couldn't keep people apart. In fact, a few Confederates found their hearts along with their bodies resting forever in Western New York, including DeWitt Clinton Guy and Philemon Tracy.

In Fairfield Cemetery, a small burial ground in the Erie Canal village of Spencerport is the grave of a soldier who fought for "the cause" and had his heart divided between the North and the South. DeWitt Clinton Guy's father was from New York state but had worked on the construction of the James River and Kanawha Canal until it reached Lynchburg, Virginia in 1840. That is where he met his wife. When the first enlargement of the Erie Canal began shortly after they were married, Guy took the opportunity to return to his home state. DeWitt was born in 1842, named after a former governor of New York and the man behind the great Erie Canal, DeWitt Clinton.

Construction on the canal was dangerous work. It claimed the lives of nearly one thousand men between 1817 and 1825, and hundred more during the expansion. The patriarch of the Guy family was one of those fatalities, killed in a cave-in while working on a lock. With the loss of her husband and no way to provide for her four children, Mrs. Guy packed up and moved them all back to Lynchburg.

Not longer after they moved, Abraham Lincoln was elected to office and the Union started to fall apart. Both sides thought that they were right and called for able-bodied men to grab arms and stand for their cause. Nineteen-year-old DeWitt Clinton Guy answered the call along with thousands of others. On April 23, 1861, he enlisted with the Eleventh Virginia Infantry, Company G. DeWitt carried a family Bible with him when he went off to war, in which he kept a journal. The first entry he wrote was about his first day on the battlefield. According to subsequent entries, he was wounded in the battles of Seven Pines in Virginia; Drewry's Bluff in Chesterfield County, Virginia; and Gettysburg, as part of Pickett's Charge. He wrote as often as he could in his sacred journal. He marched thousands of miles through the mountains of Virginia, Pennsylvania and Maryland. His final entry in his journal/Bible was made when he was held as a prisoner of war at Union-run Camp Hoffman at Lookout Point, Maryland. Confederate General Robert E. Lee surrendered to General Ulysses S. Grant at Appomattox Courthouse on April 9, 1865. And so, the war ended 3 days shy of the 4th anniversary of its beginning. Camp Hoffman closed 2 months later, and the survivors made their way back home to the arms of their loved ones.

Instead of walking toward Lynchburg, Sergeant DeWitt Clinton Guy made his way north to Ogden, New York. There was a girl waiting for him. Did I leave that part out? While his father moved the family from town to town along the Erie Canal, a special girl captured the heart of a young DeWitt and after the war, he intended to capture her hand. DeWitt courted Martha Flagg, and the young couple soon married.

The couple settled in Lynchburg to raise a family. DeWitt became a partner in a local grocery store – Bigbee, Guy and Thaxton, and a member of the masonic lodge. Their life was full of love, faith and promise, though their time together wasn't long enough. DeWitt died at the age of 46.

He had a Confederate's heart until the very end. On his deathbed in 1889, long after war was over and lost, he still claimed to be part of "Jefferson Davis's Confederacy." In his obituary published in the Lynchburg Daily Virginian on January 7, 1889, it is said that DeWitt Clinton Guy was "true to his colors and never apologized for the part he took in the lost cause." He was laid to rest at Spring Hill Cemetery. Martha was broken-hearted and returned to Ogden to be with her family. There she lived out her days until her death in 1891, just two years after her husband. Martha and DeWitt would not be apart for long. Soon after her death, his body was exhumed and made one last journey north to join Martha's eternal sleep at Fairfield Cemetery.

As for his beloved family Bible he carried in battle...it was donated to the Lynchburg Museum in November 2010 by his great-

great grandniece, where it is on display to share his story as a Confederate soldier.

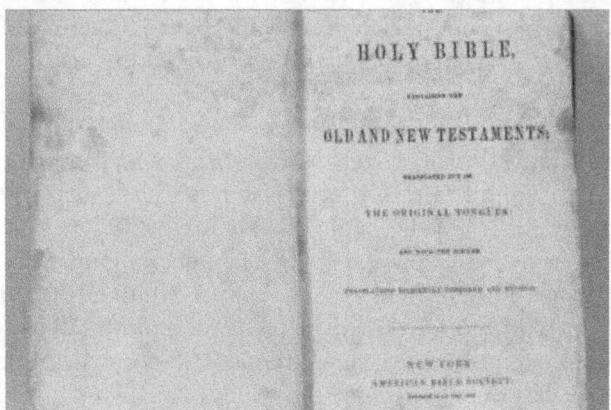
Dewitt Clinton Guy family Bible

Philemon Tracy's story is about family love and a secret burial.

Philemon Tracy was born June 27, 1831 to Edward Dorr Tracy, a Georgia Supreme Court justice, and Susan Campbell Tracy. His family was wealthy, able to send Philemon to Yale University to study law. After graduation he returned to Macon to open a law practice, he also edited the Macon Telegraph. It wasn't long before Philemon began courting Caroline Rawls, soon after they were married and were expecting to have their first child. Philemon would have his heart broken twice in one day. On March 3, 1858 Caroline died in childbirth, as did their baby. Mother and child were buried in a single casket at Rose Hill.

Now Philemon had horribly near-sighted, which should have excluded him from service, but he insisted on enlisting and fighting for the cause. Philemon entered the war as a major in the 6th Georgia Infantry. May 31st and June 1, 1862 he fought in the Battle of Seven Pines alongside his men. During the battle he was shot in the face and thigh. He was forced to convalesce at a military hospital for a couple months before rejoining General Robert E. Lee's ranks in Maryland. Shortly after the sun had risen over the fields of Antietam, Maryland, they were soaked with blook only hours after the Battle of Sharpsville had begun. At around 8:30am, a bullet entered Major Philemon's thigh and severed his femoral artery, causing him to bleed to death where he fell. The Battle of

Sharpsville was the first major battle north of the Mason-Dixon Line and the bloodiest day of the entire Civil War, leaving over 23,000 men and boys either dead or wounded. As to the death of Major Tracy, General DH Hill reported that – "The modest and heroic Major Tracy of the Sixth Georgia met there, too, a bloody grave."

As a young man, Philemon spent many summers with his uncle Phineas Tracy in Batavia, New York, who was a prominent judge and lawyer. The two had a special bond and it was no secret that Philemon was his favorite nephew. When Uncle Phineas learned that Philemon was killed and had been unceremoniously buried where he fell, he sent men to Antietam to exhume his body and bring him home to be buried in the family plot in Batavia. To ensure the safety of his nephew's remains, Phineas instructed his men to say they were transporting the body of a Union officer north.

Philemon Tracy

For decades no one knew that a rebel officer rested at the historic Batavia Cemetery on Harvester Avenue. In 1907, the Children of the Confederacy chapter in Atlanta began sending the "Stars and Bars" to decorate his grave on Memorial Day. That first year, a little girl recited "A Georgia Volunteer" by Mary Ashley Townsend at the graveside ceremony, part of which is shared below.

> *What fights he fought, what wounds he wore,*
> *Are all unknown to fame;*
> *Remember, on his lonely grave*
> *There is not e'en a name!*
> *That he fought well and bravely too,*
> *And held his country dear,*
> *We know, else he had never been*
> *A Georgia Volunteer*

On Sunday, September 16, 1990 – 128 years to the day of the eve of his death, a military marker was dedicated to the service of Major Philemon Tracy from Macon, Georgia and placed on his grave.

A TRAGIC EVENT

By the time the afternoon sun rose high in the sky on a spring day in April 1955, the first pioneers of Ogden were wiped from history...or at least their headstones were.

Destruction of the Pioneer Cemetery
Democrat & Chronicle April 3, 1955

Ogden's most famous founders are Abraham Colby, John Webster and Daniel Spencer, who had roads and even a village named after them. But the first to set foot on the town's soil were Benajah Willey and his son George. The Willey family played an important role in the establishment of Ogden and Spencerport, building the first homestead on the hill just south of the village, as well as being responsible for some historic firsts in Ogden's history.

The first frame house and barn were built by Benajah. While the first religious meeting was held in George's home in 1805. In 1815 George housed the first library within the four walls of his home, humble beginnings for the Ogden Farmer's Library.

On the family farm, George's wife Deidanna died on April 2, 1804, making her the first of the Odgen settlers to die. She was buried in a small family plot. One of the most important first, for the sake of this chapter, is the fact that Benajah Willey donated half an acre of his farmland, which encompassed that family plot, in 1808 to be used as the town's first cemetery. For fifty years the pioneers who cleared and farmed the land, opened the stores, taught in the school and saved our souls were laid to rest there. All of those who were important to the growth of the young town.

This is how a few of their stories read...

Asa Allen was born on February 16, 1797. Asa moved to Clarkson with his wife and children to become a minister in a local church. The entire family came down with a "fever," but only Asa struggled to recover. The fever turned into dropsy, which proved to be a fatal affliction. While on his deathbed he asked if he was going to die. When he was told that indeed he was, he simply said "Amen." He was only 31 years old when his light was extinguished. Asa was laid to rest in the half acre lot.

William Banning arrived in Ogden on June 9, 1803. He was responsible for planting the first orchard. Banning died on September 17, 1831, and went to eternal sleep in that sacred ground.

Dr. John Cobb graduated from Castleton Medical Center in Vermont. He served as a physician during the War of 1812 before moving to Ogden with his wife Sarah. Cobb was the first doctor in town. He had, however, a greater connection with early American history that was rooted deeper than the founding of Ogden. John Cobb was a direct descendent of Willam Bradford, governor of the Plymouth Colony in 1620 and a passenger on the Mayflower. Cobb and Sarah are both in the cemetery too, along with countless others that have made great contributions to history.

The land surrounding the cemetery changed hands several times over the years and the cemetery was referred to as both the Pioneer Cemetery and the Campion-Wright Cemetery. Regardless of what it was called, the cemetery contained the remains of some of the bravest and most hardy pioneers that laid the foundations necessary for Ogden to grow and flourish. Unfortunately, there was a time when greed overshadowed the importance of protecting legacy and respecting the memory of those who had gone before us. On April 2, 1955, 151 years after the first body was placed in the cemetery, the headstones that survived the ravages of time, the stones that marked the final resting places and the fence surrounding the hallowed ground were leveled, the earthly remains still covered with a deep blanket of soil. The record of their lives wiped away with the blade of a bulldozer to erect an appliance store. After a century and a half of being the stewards of their memory, those souls were betrayed by the all-mighty dollar.

ANYTHING IS FOSSIBLE

The following news story hit the Star-Gazette in Elmira on July 29, 1907 and caused quite the stir.

Strange Fossil Puzzles Solons
What sort of an animal has a horse-like head, tusks like a dog, long reptile body, legs like man
Seneca Falls, July 29 – Naturalists here are entirely at a loss to name the animal whose skeleton was found under a house at the corner of Haigh and Bridge Streets. The house is one of the oldest in town, and it was being repaired when the skeleton was discovered by Burt McKevitt.
The skull of the fossil is four inches long and resembles a miniature horse's head. There are tusks and grinders on the jaw. The neck is long and shaped somewhat like a horse's. The body is long and resembles that of a reptile. There are thirteen small ribs on the side and ten vertebrae in the spine below the ribs. The legs are similar to those of a human being and the feet were apparently webbed. When alive the animal probably stood a foot above the ground and was two feet long from tip to tip. There were no forefeet or signs of wings.

Though this creature remained a mystery, a month later an exciting specimen was discovered in Perkinsville, a hamlet of Wayland in Steuben County. While John Morsh was plowing his field, he stumbled on a near complete skeleton of a mastodon just a few feet below the surface at the edge of the Perkinsville swamp. Of the over 200 bones uncovered, there was a thigh bone eight feet long, four- to five-foot-long ribs and a tooth that weighed over nine pounds.

It is believed that more than 13,400 years ago, the massive animal wandered into an impenetrable swamp, sunk into the near quick sand-like ground and could not get out. The Perkinsville Mastodon is on display at the New York State Museum in Albany.

BENEATH OUR FEET THEY LIE

When New York state mandated each county to construct an almshouse in 1824, Monroe County officials did not want "those type" of people in the city; the poor, crippled, widowed, drunk and mentally ill. So, the almshouse was built about two miles outside of Rochester. It resembled a farm more than a government institution. Open land surrounded the almshouse, which allowed them to grow their own food to become somewhat self-sufficient...and bury their dead. Let's talk about their dead, shall we.

Monroe County Poorhouse

From 1847-1850 the Monroe County almshouse had seventy births and 251 deaths...in just a three-year span...251 deaths. In 1847 alone a measle outbreak claimed the lives of thirteen children all under the age of four. Twenty-five more died from "ship fever," also known as typhus, which is spread by lice, a nasty little creature that ran rampant in the close quarters. On June 4, 1848, Adonriam

Perkins died after both his legs were amputated. Six months after Perkins death, Samuel Oldinshaw succumbed to "frozen feet." The list goes on and on, with epidemic after epidemic – croup, cholera and consumption.

Thirty-seven years after the city dedicated Mount Hope Cemetery in 1838 as the official Rochester cemetery, the farm continued to inter their dead onsite, as it was a general practice for almshouses and asylums to have their own burial grounds. According to an old hand drawn map, the 175' x 125', half acre lot was located between the almshouse and penitentiary. Even though the county directors knew about the existence of the cemetery while it was in use, it was never documented on an official map. As with the cemetery adjacent to the Genesee County Poorhouse, the exact number of those laid to rest in the Rochester State Hospital cemetery will never be fully known. To say that the cemetery records were incomplete would be an understatement, they were virtually non-existent.

The 1824 law held Monroe County responsible for the care of the poor and insane. They only provided the bare minimum basic needs for them to exist. The inmates, as both the almshouse residents and patients at the asylum were call, were given a roof over their head and provided nourishment but they were never afforded the respect and compassion that every human being needed and deserved. This was true in life...and in death. The burials were performed without solemn rites and their final resting places were anonymous, with no markers.

The cemetery held the earthly remains of the deceased from the almshouse, asylum and penitentiary from 1826 to 1872. By the time of the last burial, the condition of the grounds was disgraceful. At the annual meeting of the Monroe County Board of Supervisors in January 1873, the chaplain from the almshouse gave a compelling report about how the burials took place there. "*It was not uncommon, in such cases, to make more than one attempt in opening a grave, from the pick and shovels encountering, perhaps transversely, the mouldering coffin of some convict or pauper. While in spring and autumn, in a rainy time, the wetness of the ground and water in the grave, added to the pain of dishonoring the ashes of a brother man.*" While preparing a grave for burial they would often bust into a rotting coffin of the long-since deceased due to the hap-hazard way the unmarked graves were placed. The board took the chaplain's report into consideration and ordered the use of the cemetery be suspended. They declared that all future interments be made at Mount Hope Cemetery, unfortunately, again in unmarked graves.

Decades passed and those who knew about the cemetery died off one by one. It seemed that it was very easy to forget the hundreds of bodies that lay under the ground, especially when no one cared about them when they were alive. The buildings on the farm were eventually demolished, and it became an open field. The county owned the property and in the early 1970s they decided to make it part of Highland Park.

For more than a century and a half, the bodies rested quietly under foot. Occasionally, as if asking to be remembered, bones and pieces of splintered caskets were given up by the earth. They were gathered and unceremoniously placed in a hole under a lilac tree without so much as a few words of prayer and comfort. It was not until 1984 that what the plot of land held was fully understood.

A county grounds crew was working on a landscaping project when the bulldozer operator unearthed six skeletons. The authorities were called, and construction was halted pending an investigation by the county coroner. Heavy rain fell in the days following the discovery and more remains came to the surface. A full-scale archaeological excavation was launched under the supervision of the Rochester Museum and Science Center. On the first day the remains of ten adults and two children were recovered.

"The burial ground of more than a thousand people was accidentally unearthed in what might be the largest "forgotten" cemetery in the city. (Rochester History, October 1988)" 305 complete skeletons were found, but it is believed that at least 500 to 700 more still rest in that plot of land at the corner of South and Highland Avenues.

The recovered remains were re-interred at Mount Hope Cemetery in a mass grave. Fourteen years later, those who remained in the original cemetery finally received the respect that they have always deserved. A remembrance garden was dedicated in their honor with a memorial plaque that reads; *"This plaque is dedicated to the men, women and children whose unmarked graves were discovered here in 1984. They are believed to have been 19th century residents of the Monroe County Almshouse, Insane Asylum and Penitentiary that occupied this site."*

As you visit Highland Park to take in the beautiful lilac trees and winding walking paths, take a few moments to remember those who lie beneath your feet and say a little prayer of peace for them.

CASTLE ON THE HILL

Dansville is nestled in a little valley flanked to the east and west by the foothills of the Appalachian Mountains. Like most of western New York state, the area had once been a dangerous and foreboding forest filled with British forces trying to stop the colonists from revolting and Indians who sided with the crown. Surprise attacks, often under the cover of darkness, left entire families and small communities decimated. George Washington at the time was the general in charge of all the American troops during the American Revolution. It was a war fought on two fronts. The army fought the British and the settlers clashed with the Indians. The army won battle after battle, but the settlers met defeat more than victory.

When the Revolutionary War was all but won, Washington turned his attention to avenging the murder of innocent citizens at the hands of the "savages." He ordered Generals Sullivan and Clinton to retaliate with no mercy for the Indians, as none was given to the massacred settlers. The Sullivan Expedition was a "systematic military campaign" against the four nations of the Iroquois who sided with the British crown.

On June 18, 1779, they left Fort Sullivan in Tioga, Pennsylvania and cut a path of destruction through Leicester and Canojoharie before they joined Washington and his troops in Easton, New Jersey. On their way to Leicester and Little Beard's Castle, they passed through Dansville on a footpath that followed present day Route 256 along the western shore of Conesus Lake. Near Maple Beach, a twenty-five-man detachment was ambushed by an Indian war party and fifteen of Sullivan's scouts were killed, Lieutenant Boyd and Sergeant Parker were captured and later tortured, then killed by their captors at Little Beard Castle.

The Indians that survived Sullivan and Clinton's raids either fled north to Canada or were captured and placed on reservations. As the woods were cleared, the settlers began to make their way to the western most territories of the new nation. The fear of the unknown subsided and small communities began to take hold in remote areas that were a day or two from the cities, which was the case with Dansville.

Dansville was once home to the "Castle on the Hill," a unique and interesting institution. During the spring and summer months it is hidden by dense foliage. The foothills protect its secret well. But as the leaves begin to turn to vibrant reds and oranges before falling to the ground, glimpses of the massive structure can be caught, and its full beauty is revealed.

The origin of the "castle" was built on humble beginnings. In 1796, Dansville was a small village formed by Dan Faulkner and the Pennsylvania settlers that followed. They feared God, worked hard, clung to their strict values, and believed in many superstitions and "signs." What began as a day like any other, soon turned into chaos when the ground began to shake beneath their feet. The people in the village ran up East Hill and they discovered that a spring had broken through the solid rock and water gushed out. Earthquakes did not normally happen in western New York, and they believed that the spring was brought forth by the power of God to heal the sick. The people of Dansville called it the "All-Healing Spring." The news about the spring was kept within the community, not because the people did not want to share it with outsiders, but because they were so far from the nearest city.

Nathaniel Bingham, a businessman from Rochester, heard about the spring more than fifty years after it had sprung from the hillside and made the trip to Dansville to see it for himself. Impressed by what he saw, Bingham gathered a group of investors that believed that the spring on East Hill would be a great location for a water cure.

The Europeans flocked to water cure spas, convinced that their waters cured disease and infirmities as well as revitalizing their health. During the mid-1800s there was a growing interest in alternative and holistic medicines, natures physician. Though the fascination with water and its curative power is timeless, beyond today's simple theory of drinking eight glasses a day. The earliest recorded history that people harnessed the therapeutic powers of water were discovered in Ancient Greek texts from around 2000 B.C. Hippocrates prescribed spring water baths to treat various illnesses. And the Bible also referenced it in Ezekiel 36:25 with *"I will sprinkle clean water on you, and you will be clean; I will cleanse you from all your impurities and from all your idols."* When sanitation became a problem in Medieval Europe and pure, clean water was difficult to find, the practice of hydropathy was only available for nobility. In the 18th century, doctors began in depth research into the medicinal qualities of water.

By 1850 there were 200 water cures across the United States, most run by doctors. The closest was in Avon, just twenty-eight miles away. That did not deter Bingham from opening the Dansville Water Cure. He pursued an all-out campaign to encourage people to travel to Dansville and let the water of the "All-Healing Spring" flow through them. Brochures offered testimonials by physicians, including those who invested in the Dansville Water Cure, and provided a long list of illness ranging from "hiccups to cancer" that the waters would treat. In fact, one water cure advertised that it would cure hydrophobia, (really?!?). There was no scientific studies and evidence to back up these claims. At the turn of the twentieth century, advances had been made in the sciences of pharmaceuticals and medicine that diminished the healing powers of water and the water cure spas that remained in operation became upscale vacation resorts.

Nathaniel Bingham was not a doctor, but a piano and cabinet make, just a simple businessman looking to make fast buck. The Dansville Water Cure began accepting patients in 1854 under the ownership of Bingham and his partner Lyman Granger. Unfortunately, Bingham became ill after the grand opening and had to sell his share of the business. After several owners, no one had been able to make the water cure a success until Dr. James Caleb Jackson took over in October 1858. He had a passion for hydropathy and hydrotherapy.

James Caleb Jackson had been a sickly child, and his health only worsened as he grew older. He found it difficult to work and perform the simplest of everyday tasks. Medical treatments had no effect on his condition, and he began to grasp at straws, willing to try anything. Jackson claimed that his ailments were miraculously cured after a visit to a water cure. He became a walking testimonial to the health benefits of water and its biggest advocate. Jackson attended medical school in Syracuse and then opened Glen Haven, a water cure on the shore of Skaneateles Lake. Fire destroyed the building, and his insurance policy did not cover the cost to rebuild. He was not ready to give up on his dream and seized the opportunity to buy the Dansville Water Cure. The first thing Jackson did was change the name to Our Home on the Hillside.

Throughout the history of alternative medicine, fads and advocates came and went, but Jackson was one of the most influential, especially as a nutritionist. He championed the idea of "clean eating" in the 19th century. Dr. Jackson not only promoted the benefits of hydrotherapy, but he also endorsed well-being through healthy eating habits. Our Home on the Hillside was considered a naturopathic hospital, which is defined as "*a system of treatment of disease that avoids drugs and surgery and emphasizes the use of natural agents and physical means,*" according to Merriam Webster. His health resort in the tranquil hills of the Finger Lakes region became a mecca for the rich and famous, including Frederick Douglas, Susan B. Anthony, and Horace Greeley. A visitor at the resort found that there were six things that they would not find during their stay: red meat, sugar, coffee, tea, alcohol, and tobacco. Fresh fruits, vegetables and whole grains were mainstays on the menu. Jackson spent time studying people's eating habits and found that the average diet was rich in fats and proteins, which could be linked to many of the prevalent health problems during the late-19th century. For instance, a traditional breakfast consisted of bacon or ham, meats full of salt and fat, and eggs. If he was going to make a difference in the lives if his fellow man, he decided that he needed to start with breakfast, the most important meal of the day. To get people to change their diet, he had to propose something that was easy to make and, most importantly, tasted good. Jackson invented the first "ready to eat" cold cereal. He took advantage of the abundance of locally grown grains, and mixed bran from the grains, graham flour and water, then baked it. He called it granula. Before going to bed, the granula was broken into nuggets and soaked in milk overnight.

Shortly after granula made its debut, Dr. John Harvey Kellogg paid Our Home on the Hillside a visit in 1878 after he got a tip from a member of his church in Michigan. Kellogg wanted to see what Jackson did at his spa, in the name of "science," and Jackson was more than happy to share his theories with a fellow physician. Jackson shared too much information with Kellogg. About two years after his visit, Kellogg marketed his own cereal also called granula. When news of the copycat cereal reached Jackson, he quickly filed an infringement lawsuit against his rival. The case was ruled in Jackson's favor, and Kellogg was forced to change the name of his cereal to granola. In 1897, the field of competition grew when C.W. Post introduced Grapenuts to market shelves.

After the lawsuit was settled, James Caleb Jackson made the decision to retire and pass the water cure business down to his children. Even though he was not responsible for the day-to-day operation of Our Home on the Hillside, he was never far from the action. The family-owned Brightside, a property across the street, and this became the Jackson patriarch's home until he passed away on July 11, 1895.

It wasn't long after the children took control of the water cure that tragedy struck. At the time there was no electricity at Our Home on the Hillside, that was not uncommon in rule areas. Lanterns and candles were used throughout the building for lighting. While everyone was asleep on the evening of June 26, 1882, a lantern overturned in the room of a patient. The kerosene spilled out and ran along the floorboards, allowing the flames to quickly spread. By the time the firemen arrived on scene, there was no way that the building could be saved. Instead, they concentrated on preventing the fire from spreading to other buildings on the property. By the time the sun rose on over the crest of the hill, the wooden building had been reduced to ashes and charred beams. The building may have been destroyed however, no one was injured or killed.

The June 27, 1882 edition of *The Daily News* in Batavia reported on the fire.

Danville's Water Cure Burned

The explosion of a kerosene lamp in the room of a patient at "Our Home on the Hillside" at Dansville set the building on fire last night and it burned to the ground in an incredibly short space of time. The inmates were all removed safely and were cared for in the surrounding cottages, the seminary, and the village hotels. The loss on buildings and contents is estimated at $50,000, and a large number of persons are thrown out of employment. It will probably be rebuilt.

Reports of the fire were seen in newspapers as far away as Harrisburg, Pennsylvania on June 28, 1882. This is how the brief article read.

Fire at a Sanitary Institution

Dansville, N.Y., June 28 – The water cure establishment of Dr. Jas. C. Jackson, known as "Our Home on the Hillside," in this place, took fire at one o'clock yesterday morning and was totally destroyed. The fire was caused by the explosion of a lamp in the room of one of the patients. All the inmates escaped.

As the smoke cleared, plans were made to quickly rebuild. A year later a five-story brick building stood where the pile of rubble had been. The grand opening was held on October 1, 1883, twenty-five years to the day that their father introduced the world to Our Home on the Hillside. With the rebirth of the building came a new name as well, and it would now be known as the Jackson Sanitarium.

Jackson Sanitarium rebuilt after the fire

A new name was not the only changes that were made. They expanded the services offered there as well as launched the Jackson Sanitarium Training School for Nurses, which graduated their first class in 1904. Though it did not matter what changes were made; "modern medicine" was beginning to evolve. Advances in medicine and pharmacology offered people new treatment ideas and hope. It put public faith back into traditional medicine and people began to turn away from alternative and holistic options. It was a slow death for the Jackson Sanitarium and its doors closed in 1914 and it sat empty for two years.

William Leffingham, a shrewd businessman, became the new owner and with that a new chapter in the building's history began. The United States had been drawn into World War I and the need for hospitals stateside to treat the soldiers when they returned grew. Leffingham had what the government needed, a large building that could easily transform into a military hospital and the United States Army signed a contract to use the property as General Hospital No. 13. When it opened in November 1918 between 100 and 200 soldiers were treated there for psychoneurosis, or PTSD. The military headquarters in Washington, D.C. conducted an audit that found services were duplicated at some of the facilities and many of the hospitals were no longer needed. That was bad news for Leffingham and the town of Dansville. General Hospital No. 13 served 368 soldiers and four months after it opened, the hospital was shuttered on March 19, 1919.

The future of the old Jackson Sanitarium was uncertain, for a decade the halls of the massive building were quiet. Bernarr MacFadden breathed new life into it in the spring 1929. Just like James Caleb Jackson, Bernarr was sickly from the moment he was born. At age eleven, he was an orphan placed on a farm by the state. There he quickly discovered that physical labor and the wholesome, farm-grown food made him healthier and stronger. This moment of enlightenment sparked his passion to share with the world his fitness beliefs and become one of America's top experts on healthy living.

MacFadden was a health fanatic, professional wrestler, body builder, and publisher of the magazine *Physical Culture*, after which he named his latest acquisition, Jackson Sanitarium. His emphasis on a healthy diet was like that of Dr. Jackson. MacFadden's hotel offered an array of activities for his guests, which included tennis, swimming, hiking and golf. They could also take advantage of the many therapeutic treatments made available to them as well.

Bernarr was a very wealthy and popular man, as the list of his friends and acquaintances reflected. Many would visit his Western New York resort from time to time. It was common to see senators, political powerhouses, Hollywood stars and socialites in downtown Dansville. It did not take long for the Physical Culture Hotel to become a popular getaway for the rich and famous, even in the years of the Great Depression.

Shortly after the Physical Culture hotel opened, MacFadden, along with a crowd of his followers, would embark on marches that lasted upwards of two weeks to promote his regiment of a diet consisting of an enzyme-rich, raw food diet and exercise. The marches would depart from New York City, Philadelphia or Cleveland and arrive hundreds of miles later at the hotel in

Dansville. The newspapers dubbed them "Cracked Wheat Derbies" because the only food eaten on these hikes was a mixture of cracked wheat, grapefruit, raisins, honey, and brown sugar. As the marching travelers approached Dansville, they would meet with a reception fit for royalty that included a huge meal and celebration.

The *Wayne County Times* reported in their June 24, 1937 edition of the arrival of a MacFadden march in Dansville. This is how it read.

Score another triumph for Bernarr MacFadden and his 48 men and women guests who leisurely strolled the highway 325 miles from Broadway to Dansville, arriving at Physical Culture Hotel on the hillside overlooking Dansville Friday, June 4, where a distinguished reception committee welcomed them into the Genesee country.

Virtually all the hikers had discarded pairs of shoes. Shoe tops had been cut away to create a sandal-effect and ease foot sores. Blisters, with few exceptions, however, had become calloused after the first few days.

MacFadden, a vocal and charismatic character, was quoted with the following statement after the group he led returned from a Cracked Wheat Derby that started in Cleveland, Ohio. *"They've found the fountain of youth. It flows in our feet. I wish every man and woman could learn that. Nobody needs any gland transplantation, any operation, to become young again. He needs only walk. These people are proof of that statement. Talk to some of them and you'll be convinced."*

Throughout his lifetime, Bernarr MacFadden embarked on many business ventures, some failed and others were a success. The Physical Culture hotel was one of the successes. When he died in 1955 at the age of 87, William Fromcheck, a New York City hotelier, bought MacFadden's hotel and continued to operate it as a health spa, renaming it Bernarr MacFadden's Castle on the Hill. Fromcheck lacked the passion that Bernarr had for it and the hotel began to lose ground. When the Castle on the Hill closed at the end of the summer season 1971 it never opened again.

Five decades of harsh Western New York winters and neglect have taken a toll on the majestic brick "castle." Many of the buildings have fallen victim to vandals and arson by those who have no respect for their wonderful history. What they have not destroyed, Mother Nature slowly reclaims as her own.

COME HELL OR HIGH WATER

The summer 1863 was a wet one, the northeastern portion of the United States was inundated with heavy rains. Creeks and rivers swelled at an alarming rate and soon spilled over their banks which sent torrents of water downstream that left an impressive swath of destruction.

Concerns began to grow on July 21st in Moravia, Cayuga County about Dry Creek, which ran through the village. Torrential rains had pounded the already saturated ground for more than 24 hours and the water kept rising. Around 10am, their worst fears materialized. Water filled with uprooted trees and debris raced downstream toward the village destroying bridges, dams and buildings along the way. In no time Moravia was covered by two or three feet of water. The foaming rapids cut through the gravel and quicksand along the banks of Dry Creek like a hot knife through butter. It took less than an hour for nearly 40 graves in Dry Creek Cemetery to be ripped from their final resting places.

The following article appeared in the August 3, 1863 edition of the Philadelphia Press – *"A cemetery washed away – A sad incident of the severe rainstorm of last Tuesday, which was felt with more or less force over most of the state, was in the washing away of portions on the graveyard in Moravia, Cayuga County, NY. It is being rumored in the village that Dry Creek, swollen beyond all precedent, was fast undermining the western portions of the cemetery, a large crowd hastened thither, with spades and shovels, in hope that they might exhume the remainder of their friends ere the water could reach them. But the hope was in vain, and coffin after coffin was seen to be washed from its resting place, mingling promiscuously with stumps, trees and driftwood of every description. About an acre of soil was washed away to the depth of twenty feet, and as some of the coffins fell out, the rough boxes would strike on end, burst and leave an exposed coffin, the cover of which coming off; its contents would pitch headlong into the torrent...*

One of the coffins washed away in the flood was that of Lieutenant Stoyell, who was buried just a few weeks prior. George Cobb Stoyell was one of the brave fighting men with E Company of the New York 9th heavy artillery, one of the most gallant regiments from New York state. At the age of 24, Stoyell died in a Georgetown, Washington DC military hospital on June 21, 1863. His body was brought home to be buried at Dry Creek Cemetery. *The Historical Sketches of Moravia* documented the rescue of Stoyell's remains. *"A rope was immediately procured from the house of Philip Ercanbrock, and an attempt made to secure the remains, but before this could be done the embankment again went down, and they were precipitated a distance of twenty-five feet into the flood below.*

It is impossible to describe the feelings of the witnesses of this terrible scene, who, powerless to save, saw the remains of one – a few months previous was their associate and friend, so ruthlessly unearthed and swept wildly down the watery current. The box in which the coffin was enclosed, however, firmly built, and without receiving material injury, was cast upon a bank of sand which had been thrown up in the midst of the stream just above the plank road. Here another attempt was made to rescue the body, by the aide of a rope, one end of which was firmly held by two of the party and grasp by the other who plunged into the water, but was instantly swept away from the rope and down the stream with great force, and only escaped destruction by catching and clinging to willow branches overhanging the creek, until rescued."

Stoyell's coffin was recovered undamaged, while others that had been in the ground for decades did not fare as well. Coffins burst open by the incredible pressure of the floodwaters, casting their bones into the rapids. In all, sixteen coffins had been carried beyond the rescuers' hands, a week later only eight had been recovered. Bones were scattered along the creek bank like carelessly discarded driftwood.

The remains recovered, including those of Lieutenant Stoyell, as well as the damaged graves were reinterred a few months later when Indian Mound Cemetery was dedicated.

THE CURSE OF DEVIL'S NOSE

Lake Ontario and the topography of the shoreline was carved by receding glacial ice over 11,000 years ago. What was left behind were deep lakes, high bluffs, and sandy beaches that have been finely sculpted by thousands of years of gentle waves and furious winter storms. Devil's Nose is one of the bluffs formed by the glacial ice. It sits on the western edge of Hamlin Beach State Park about twenty miles west of the Port of Rochester. The steep, sandy, forty-foot-high bluff is just a fraction of the size it once was, as the rising lake levels and wind erosion have slowly eaten it away. And although the shifting sands make to bluff unstable, what lies beneath the surface of the water is the real danger. A rocky, clay shoal nearly a mile long stretches out from the shore where it waits to trap unsuspecting ships. According to oceantreasures.org; *The Coast Pilot, which was once the Bible of navigators, warned sailors to keep half a mile offshore for good water as there was a 'dirty spur' almost a mile east of Devil's Nose with only a foot of draft on it, roughly three-eights of a mile out.*

From the mid-eighteenth to the early-twentieth century, ships that sailed on the Great Lakes kept within a mile or two off the shore during rough and stormy weather. In fact, if they encountered a blinding snowstorm or squall, it was common practice to keep half a mile from shore to keep track of land and prevent the crew from becoming disoriented. Though it was a common practice, it was not always a safe one. As unassuming as the waters near Devil's Nose appeared, when the lake became angry the churning water would break against the rocks that jutted out from the shoal and Devil's Nose earned the moniker of "ship graveyard."

The first ship sailed the waters of the Great Lakes shortly after the British established the colonies in North America. *Le Griffon* launched in 1679 on the Niagara River. And with the first ship to sail came the first shipwreck, on Lake Michigan, the same year, though its identity is unknown. In fact, for each shipwreck recorded on logs and journals, there is a ship that slipped below the surface unrecorded.

British soldiers, the *Duchess of York* carried passengers and a variety of cargo. She inadvertently passed over the shoals and became stuck on the rocks during a furious November gale in 1799. The ship was doomed to break apart as the powerful waves crashed against the hull, so the passengers and crew boarded the deck boat to set sail to Kingston, Ontario, Canada. The fate of the *Duchess of York* was reported to newspaper readers across the region, as the *Niagara Constellation* out of Niagara-on-Lake did on December 7, 1799. *On Thursday last, November 29th, a boat arrived here from Schenectady. She passed the York, sticking on a rock off Devil's Nose. No prospect of getting her off.* And according to the *Upper Canada Gazette* on December 21, 1799 – *We hear from a very good authority that the schooner York, Captain Murray, has floundered and is cast upon the American shore about 50 miles from Niagara, where the captain and his men are encamped. Mr. Joseph Forsyth, one of the passengers, hired a boat to carry them to Kingston.* The luck of the passengers on the deck boat would prove to be nothing but bad. Just twelve miles from Oswego, the boat sprung a leak. As the last passenger was rescued by a passing ship, it sank like a rock to the bottom of the lake. One could say that luck was on the passengers' side, and they could say that they survived two sinking ships within a matter of days.

The schooner *C Reeve* left Chicago with 13,500 bushels of corn in November 1862 headed for Oswego. The *Exchange* departed Oswego for Lake Erie ports with a hull full of Onondaga salt. Late in the afternoon of November 22nd, a strong wind blew from the north that brought a blinding snowstorm with near zero visibility. Neither ship saw the other as they approached Devil's Nose until the *Exchange* rammed into the side of the *C Reeve* and left a hole in her hull. Within minutes she sank. Even though the *Exchange* was also damaged, they were able to bring the *C Reeve's* crew aboard before limping back to the port at Charlotte. The *Rochester Union and Advertiser* reported that when the *Exchange* docked, she *"bears the marks of a collision and reminds one of a bully with his nose badly broken."*

The *Undine* also met her fate at Devil's Nose on November 1, 1890. Headed for Sodus, the two-masted schooner was full of coal when she was caught in a winter gale. The hull dragged across the shoal and ripped a hole in the bottom. Water rushed in faster than the pumps could handle, and the *Undine* sank where she sat. The crew boarded a yawl and sailed twenty miles to Charlotte.

The last ship to fall victim to the hidden rocks at Devil's Nose was the *Reuben Doud* in 1903. Even though Devil's Nose claimed its last, the icy depths of the other lakes in the Great Lakes chain continued to take their prey to this day.

CUYLERVILLE'S NATIONAL HOTEL

According to the National Park Service, the Erie Canal opened in 1825 to revolutionize trade, commerce and transportation, as well as opening the western frontier to the more industrialized eastern seaboard. With the Erie Canal's success in the first decade, other canals were built to tie into it and further the growth of trade and the economy. Construction of the Genesee Valley Canal began in 1836, which would connect the Alleghany River in Olean to the Erie Canal and opened trade between Rochester, New York and Pittsburgh, Pennsylvania. Some of the towns along the canals were built because of it, while older towns reaped the benefits that business on the canal brought. Cuylerville witnessed the changes to the country as the American Revolution ended and national industrialization began, including the construction of the Genesee Valley Canal.

Cuylerville was once the site of Little Beard's Town or Chenussio, a powerful Seneca Indian village. The destruction of Chenussio was order by George Washington in retaliation for the brutal torture of Lieutenant Boyd and Sergeant Parker when they were ambushed by a party of renegades in 1779. (But that is a story in and of itself for another time and another book.) The Native Americans that survived the attack by Sullivan's Expedition were moved to the reservation near Cuba, New York. And as soon as the smoke cleared, settlers began to move in. Cuylerville was officially incorporated 60 years later in 1840.

The National Exchange, presently the National Hotel, was built in 1837 by Charles Phinney a few years before the Genesee Valley Canal opened. A stagecoach stopped at the hotel twice a week and when the canal opened, the business opportunities were numerous. The National Exchange housed and fed travelers from all over the country.

There was a difference between the caliper of a person that rode the stagecoach and those who worked on the canal. The captain and the crew were hired based on their reputation for being able to get the job done. Competition for freight contracts was fierce, which meant that only the toughest and most ruthless men were employed by the freight companies. Police blotters and newspapers were filled with reports of fights, and sometimes murders, at the docks and taverns. It was known that a drunk canaler was a dangerous one. The following story occurred at the National Exchange when the canal first opened.

The first boat to be pulled down the canal when it opened on September 1, 1840 from Rochester to Mt. Morris was piloted by Bucko Ben Streeter, known as the Terror of the Valley and the Rochester Bully. He has recently fought for a straight hour in the old Rochester Reynolds Arcade with a negro named Sleepy Frank. On the second boat pulled in the Cuylerville Basin in front of the hotel was Bucko Ben's old opponent Sleepy Frank. "Let's get this damn thing over with," yelled Bucko Ben and he stripped to the waist. The only rule was that the loser had to buy five rounds of drinks for the house. The fight began in the hotel bar and ended in the horse stables, lasted two hours and it was Bucko Ben who bought the drinks. He never returned to Rochester, sold his boat and became a law-abiding citizen of Cuylerville."

Truesdale Lamson ran the National Exchange for Phinney in 1843. Lamson was known to be a staunch abolitionist, and the hotel became a stop on the Underground Railroad during his time as manager. James G. Birney, Liberty Party presidential nominee in 1840 and 1844, also moved slaves through the hotel. The attic and stairwell were perfect hiding places for runaway slaves. At the height of the movement in 1848 alone, twenty-eight slaves used the National Exchange on their journey to freedom.

It only took ten years after the Genesee Valley Canal opened for Cuylerville to become an important port. Within that decade, the town's business center boomed to include several stores and warehouses. Farmers to the south and west brought their produce to the canal landing in order the ship it to the markets in Rochester. The success of the canal meant success for the National Hotel as well. A steady increase in traffic on the canal and stage route brought more business and with the hotel less than fifty yards from the canal basin, there was never a shortage of clientele. To better serve their visitors, they began to distill whiskey on site to help quench their thirst...at the same time William B. Wooster taught

Sunday School in one of the gathering halls. One stop for sin and forgiveness.

In early America inns, hotels and taverns wore many hats in their communities. The National Hotel was not only an inn, but it was also the town meeting hall and boasted a visit from William H. Seward prior to the opening shots of the Civil War. Seward was a politician from Auburn, New York who aspired to become President of the United States. Abraham Lincoln beat him in the race but chose Seward to serve as his Secretary of State for both terms.

Thousands of miles of track were laid across the country and transit times for commerce were drastically cut and it was soon apparent that the canal could not compete with the railroad and the Genesee Valley Canal was closed in 1877. Cuylerville, especially the National Hotel, took a crippling hit. By the turn of the 20th century Cuylerville's town government dissolved and it became a hamlet of Leicester. The town may have been dealt, what seemed at the time, a death blow, the hotel got a new breath of life when the Pennsylvania Railroad bought the canal path and laid down tracks for a branch with a station directly across the street from the National Hotel.

The Sterling Salt Mine opened in 1906 and once again Cuylerville was booming. Immigrants, mostly from Italy, began to stream in to work at the mine and the National Hotel would become a boarding house for some of the miners and their families. According to newspapers like the *Livingston Republican*, the hotel became the center of a bootleg liquor ring during prohibition. Another newspaper reported in August 1925 that a large amount illegal alcohol was destroyed during a police raid. It was even rumored that the hotel had ties with the mob.

The mine closed in 1930 and Cuylerville's rebirth was short-lived. The National Hotel tried to stay in business as long as it could. As the popularity of the automobile grew, fewer people traveled by train. For a while, those touring by car sustained them, but barely. Then those few patrons disappeared when the United States was drawn into WWII and gasoline was in short supply. The doors of the hotel closed for the first time, but not for long.

Construction of the Mt. Morris Dam began in 1948 and the hotel had a reason to open. Engineers and out-of-town workers would need a place to eat and sleep. As the country saw an economic upturn, once again the National Hotel would become a destination.

After 167 years of business, the National Hotel was added to the National Registry of Historic Places in 2004. You can no longer spend the night at the hotel, but it is worth the drive for a four-star dining experience.

DAREDEVILS AND SHOWMEN

There has never been a time when Americans were not obsessed with daredevils and sideshow freaks. And what child hasn't dreamt of running away with the circus. In fact, on an episode of *Little House on the Prairie*, Albert Ingalls tried to do just that. It's all about the thrill. Today we push the envelope as far as we can for the thrill of it; it was much the same in the nineteenth and early-twentieth centuries. These historic figures pushed their envelopes farther than anyone had done before, and the public ate every bit of it up. As long as someone was willing to perform, the crowds were guaranteed to come.

The first recorded American daredevil was the "Yankee Leaper," better known to Western New Yorkers as Sam Patch. Patch was born in 1799 in Pawtucket, Rhode Island. At the time when child labor laws had not been given a thought, he worked as a mule spinner at Slater Mill. A mule spinner's job was to reach into the spinning machine to untangle threads and tie the broken ones together. As a young boy he made his first jump in his hometown. Patch and his friends swam in the waters of the millrace, and he often jumped from the milldam. As they got older, they would jump off a bridge into the Blackstone River, each trying to outdo and impress the others. Patch looked for higher perches to dive from, and few boys were brave enough to leap from the heights that he did.

What started as boyhood antics soon began to draw crowds of people. He continued his daring jumps forever upping the ante. When Patch moved to Paterson, New Jersey he found work at a local mill. Then around twenty-seven years old, the young man had not outgrown his penchant for death-defying jumps into the turbulent waters below. When it was announced that a bridge was being built across the Passaic River, he vowed to make it his next feat. It would be his highest jump to date. People in Paterson, and the surrounding area, enjoyed watching the construction of the bridge. Patch used that to his advantage. He chose September 29,

1827, which was the date workers were set to place the bridge over the Great Passaic Falls. Police were on the lookout for Patch, but he eluded them. He appeared on a precipice at the falls and addressed the crowd. Patch then removed his coat, vest and shoes which he folded carefully beside him. After a brief pause, he shot feet first 80 feet down into the churning waters. A few moments later, he broke the surface of the water. The legend of the Yankee Leaper was officially born.

Addicted to the admiration and adrenaline rush, he set his sights on bigger targets. Two years later, Patch found himself standing about the churning currents of Niagara Falls on a platform built on Goat Island. The *Colonial Advocate* reported on his October 7, 1829 jump - *He walked out clad in white, and with great deliberation out his hands close to his side and jumped from the platform into the midst of the vast gulf of foaming water from which none of human kind had ever emerged in life.*

Emerged he did. Sam Patch was the first to survive such a stunt. The *Buffalo Republican* shared with its subscribers that *the jump of Patch is the greatest feat of the kind ever effected by man. He may now challenge the universe for a competitor.*

No one dared to take the challenge, so Patch bested himself. Ten days later, he jumped again from the platform set even higher above the falls at a dizzying 125 feet. The crowd was not disappointed.

Now, you need to understand that an adrenaline junkie is never satisfied and is always looking for a new high, the next rush. Patch and his new pet black bear headed east to Rochester, New York. Advertisements in the Rochester paper set the date and time of his next jump as November 6, 1829 at 2:00 pm. For the first time his bear was jumping with him. Before a crowd of eight thousand, they stood on a platform ninety-seven feet above the Genesee River at High Falls. Patch pushed his bear from the platform and then followed him into the turbulent water. Another successful leap. Even though there was a big crowd, the payout was not what Patch expected. Money was the sole reason why he decided to give a repeat performance a week later.

Greed makes man blind and foolish, and makes him an easy prey for death - Rumi

Posters and advertisements for his second jump on November 13th were plastered all over the city. They promised that Patch would perform a more daring feat as "Sam's Last Jump," which certainly at press time meant that it was his last jump of the season. The platform had been raised to 125 feet. Before taking the leap, Patch gave a speech to the crowd which ended with "Napolean was a great man and a great general. He conquered nations, but he couldn't jump the Genesee Falls."

And with that, he and his bear jumped from the platform. What happened next was unclear, but something went horribly wrong. Did he hit the rocks that jutted from gorge wall on the way down? Or did he just hit the water too hard? Some said Patch was drunk when he left the platform. The only thing that everyone could agree on was that Sam Patch did indeed leave the platform and plummet 125 feet to the water below. The crowd had held its collective breath for what seemed like an eternity, but Patch never surfaced. His advertisement proved to be prophetic. On a side note, November 13, 1829 was a Friday. Perhaps his luck had simply run out.

On November 14, 1829, New York's *Saturday Evening Post* gave Sam Patch a glowing review. *The now distinguished name of Sam Patch, which erst had never been pronounced out of the little town of Paterson, is rapidly running the honorable circle of newspaper eulogy, from Maine to Georgia. Wherever Sam goes, he meets with welcome! The good people of every town anticipates his arrival, and not a man, woman, or child are content, till they hear from his lips that there is no mistake.* When the paper hit the streets on the morning of the 14th, Sam Patch was dead. Neither the reporter or editor had any idea of his death when it went to print.

A few months later, his body was found frozen downstream in the ice at Charlotte, near the shore of Lake Ontario. His bear was never found. He was buried in Charlotte Cemetery on River Street without the pomp and circumstance befitting a famous entertainer. A wooden marker on his grave read "Sam Patch – Such is Fame." After 195 years, the wooden marker is gone, as is the exact location of the Yankee Leaper's final resting place. According to the April 1925 obituary of Mary Ann Davis, the ninety-five-year-old woman was the last living person who knew where Patch rests.

When Sam Patch died during his last jump, local clergy and a select few blamed the spectators for his death. The Anti-Mason Enquirer said it was "a daring and useless exposure of human life that left the crowd abashed and rebuked after seeing frail mortal, standing, as it proved, on the brink of eternity."

It would be decades before a new daredevil captured the region's attention the way that Sam Patch had. A gentleman by the name of Jean Francois Gravelet Blondin was responsible for re-igniting the fire. And all he did was stretch a rope high above Niagara Falls and walk it. After that, a new breed of daredevil was born to entertain the masses.

The banks of the Genesee River had developed since Sam's final show. Falls Field sat on the eastern side of the river gorge near present-day Platt Street. N.P. Demarest, owner of Falls Field, always looked for a gimmick that would bring more business to his saloon and beer garden. To capitalize on the popularity of Blondin's recent stunt, he brought French tightrope walker Anloise de Lave to Rochester. De Lave laid his rope across the gorge 110 feet above the river, ready to perform. His first walk on August 16, 1859 drew a crowd of over 18,000 people which filled all the hotel rooms in the city and gave the local taverns and restaurants a windfall. He amazed thousands every day for two weeks with his dangerous and daring tricks. Each walk was a two-for-one, a bargain for twenty-five cents; de Lave crossed the gorge and then turned around and crossed it again. Each trip across the rope featured different stunts so that no two days were the same. People saw as many performances as their wallets and change purses would allow.

While de Lave's performances were entertaining, their drew criticism from the clergy, just as Sam Patch's jumps did. Young men and boys tried to imitate the stunts de Lave performed, many were injured – some seriously. Despite the backlash from some, the daily performances continued. The last of his walks was the most daring of them all. Robert Smith, a local man from Rochester, volunteered to be carried by de Lave...high above the falls...from one side of the gorge to the other. As they slowly and carefully made their way across, de Lave slipped and both men fell. The crowd drew a collective breath and held it. Fortunately, the men had the presence of mind to grab hold of the rope and make their way, hand over hand, to land. Both men lived to tell their grandchildren of their harrowing experience; however, a spectator fell over the edge into the gorge and was instantly killed.

At the same time de Lave was walking the rope in Rochester, 19 miles to the west two young men thrilled the masses in Brockport. For the Cornes and Parker rope walking exhibition, they crossed over the Erie Canal between the Holmes House and the American Hotel. Before a crowd of hundreds of people, Cornes and Parker walked towards each other from opposite sides of the canal. When they met in the middle, Cornes lay on the rope as Parker stepped over him. Their stunts went off without a hitch.

Three months after Blondin crossed Niagara Falls, "tightrope fever" continued to spread across the countryside of Western New York. First Rochester, westward to Brockport and then Albion. At the time, the Orleans County Fair was held in Albion, instead of Knowlesville as it is today. On September 28, 1859, during the fair, a daredevil from Brockport strung his rope from the second floor of the Mansion Hotel across the canal to the second floor of Pierpont Dryer's building. Hundreds of people lined the canal bank and streets. But the premium viewing spot was on the three-arched drawbridge on Main Street, where more than 250 people and a few horses packed on the iron deck. As the rope walker started out the window of the Mansion House, the bridge began to moan and strain under the incredible weight of the crowd unit it finally collapsed. The canal was filled with bodies. Those who could swim made it to shore, where the onlookers pulled them onto the bank. Others were trapped under the bodies of fellow townspeople and horses. At the end of the day, at least fifteen people were dead, mostly children, and scores were injured. Nearly a century and a half later in 2002, a marker was erected by the Orleans County Historical Society was a solemn reminder of that day.

In 1886 Blondin was interested in beginning another American tour, but he felt that a new law in Niagara Falls which required safety nets would draw smaller crowds and less money. However, the law wasn't adopted everywhere and the dangerous feats continued.

A strange and unfortunate accident happened at the July 9, 1892 performance of Professor Le Carte in Glen Haven. Sixty-three feet above the ground before a crowd of 500, Le Carte successfully traversed the rope and started his backward walk. A quarter of the way back, one of the guy wires gave way, which caused Le Carte to lose balance and fall. On the way down his chin caught a guy wire causing him to somersault and shoot straight down. He landed on his feet, sinking into the soft sod. Miraculously he suffered no broken bones, only a badly bruised chin.

Acts from extreme heights weren't limited to the tight rope. Balloonist Carrie Myers, aka Mrs. WH Wilcox, stunned crowds at fairs with a new death-defying stunt. A stunt that made it look like Sam Patch jumped into puddles from the front porch step. Myers ascended 700 feet in the air in the basket of a balloon. She then strapped on a parachute, stood on the edge of the basket and descended into the crowd below. At the Olean Racetrack on September 14, 1907, something went terribly wrong. After Myers left the basket a gust of wind picked up, tangling her parachute chords which caused her parachute to fail. She hit the ground at 120mph. Every bone in Myers body shattered on impact. Thankfully her death was instantaneous and painless, though the sheer terror she felt must have been imaginable.

It seemed that there was no shortage of opportunities to quench the public's thirst for a thrill. When the daredevils left town, the circus arrived. Dozens of circus troupes crisscrossed the country in the late-1800s. Late at night, circus wagons and trains pulled into Rochester and quickly began to set up the Big Top at Falls Field. Though they arrived under the cover of darkness, the word traveled fast. By mid-morning Rochesterians lined the streets waiting for the parade...there was always a parade. It was the most anticipated part of the circus. It gave people who could not afford the price of a ticket a chance to enjoy a small part of it all. The Rochester Republican wrote this about Spaulding's Monster Circus, *"The unparalleled celebrity of the company and the magnificent spectacle presented by their triumphal procession in the morning drew together a crowd...never before witnessed at one time under one pavilion...not less than four thousand persons, many of them consisting of groups of ladies and gentlemen who for the first time now attended a circus."*

PT Barnum brought his Barnum's Greatest Show on Earth to Rochester. Trumpeting elephants and a lively steam calliope, which could reportedly be heard twelve miles away, announced their arrival. An article in an 1868 edition of the Union and Advertiser described *"the colossal lionine car, bearing beautiful women, in the center of which a large living lion, uncaged and unchained reposed in all his majesty near his keeper."*

In the mid-nineteenth century, circuses usually had just plays, animals, equestrians and acrobats. It was PY Barnum who introduced sideshow acts, which would become synonymous with the circus. One of the side show attractions that became part of the Barnum Cirus was a replica of Western New York's Cardiff Giant.

The "petrified giant" was the brainchild of George Hull, an atheist who came up with the idea of a fake giant after losing an argument with Reverend Turk about the Biblical existence of giants on earth in Genesis 6:4. It was Hull's stance that Christians would fall for anything. His plan was very ingenious and involved several lies inside of lies and sworn oaths of secrecy.

He and HB Martin hired men from a quarry in Fort Dodge, Iowa to cut a 10 foot 4 ½ inch block of gypsum under the guise that it was for a monument of Abraham Lincoln. It was then sent to a German stonecutter in Chicago named Edward Burghardt, who ordered his associates to carve it under cover in the likeness that looked more like Hull than Lincoln. When the "giant" was finished, it was then taken east by train and buried in November 1868 on the farm of his cousin William Newell. For a year it sat buried until October 16, 1869 for the next phase of the hoax. Newell hired Gideon Emmons and Henry Nichols to dig a well. When the "giant' was unearthed, one of the men declared, *"Some old Indian had been buried here."*

A tent was erected over the dig site and Newell charged fifty cents for a 15-minute look at the "discovery." Within days hundreds of people descended on Cardiff, New York and filled the hotels and restaurants.

Theories of its origin changed almost as many times as ownership. PT Barnum was impressed by the number of people the Cardiff Giant drew and offered $50,000 for it but was turned down. So, Barnum had a wax/plaster replica made and took the giant on the road.

People began to crave more thrills like this, becoming "circus mad." They flocked to freak shows and side shows, shelling out their hard-earned money for a chance to peek in a tent and catch a glimpse of the Wild Boy of India who was raised by wolves, the Fiji Mermaid and other exotic and bizarre spectacles. Curiosity emporiums, museums of the odd and macabre began to spring up across the country in general stores and tavern backrooms everywhere, ready to feed the fascination one nickel at a time. One man came to Rochester to set up his show and became a local icon.

Rattlesnake Pete, born Peter Gruber in 1858 in Oil City, Pennsylvania, was the son of an oil refiner. He had always been obsessed with snakes and reptiles. At a young age, Peter learned from the local Seneca Indians how to catch rattlesnakes, copperheads and other adders. From their medicine woman, he learned how to use the serpents to make medicines and antidotes, as well as clothing from the skins. Keeping with native traditions, no part of the animal was wasted.

When Peter's father left the oil business, he and Peter opened a restaurant/saloon with a museum on the side. In 1892, Oil City, which is ninety miles north of Pittsburgh, fell to disaster. Floods plagued the city, which were then followed by explosive fires that destroyed what the water had not. The city was in ruin, including the Gruber saloon. With nothing left at home, Peter headed north and soon found himself in Rochester.

Once in Rochester, he opened a saloon and curiosity emporium at 8-10 Mill Street behind Reynolds Arcade. In his emporium, he not only had snakes and reptiles, but also a vast collection of strange items bordering on the macabre. Rattlesnake Pete's collection included the corpse of a petrified woman, the battle flag from Custer's last stand, and what he claimed to be one of the very first electric chairs. Pete also was said to have personal belongings of John Wilkes Booth and the James brothers, as well as the very weapon used by a wife-killing axe murderer.

He sold venom and oils from the snake she captured, as well as things he made from them. True to his nickname, Rattlesnake Pete not only kept the slithering creatures, but he also dressed from head to toe in their skins. According to stories passed down throughout the years, he once saved a circus clown who had been bitten by a rattlesnake. Pete also treated hundreds of people with goiters by wrapping his snakes around their necks; the gentle, massaging movements of the snake's muscles relieved their discomfort. In Arch Merrill's *Rochester Scrapbook,* the author further relayed Rattlesnake Pete's place in the community, *"Whenever any strange animals showed up in Rochester, Pete was sent for...to pick up sinister lizards from banana shipments in the railroad yards, to capture monkeys escaped from a carnival, to kill snakes, invariably harmless ones that householders found in their cellars."* Pete was a Victorian version of Billy the Exterminator.

He was quite the character and marched to the beat of his own drum. Peter Gruber died on October 11, 1932. His collection was auctioned off after his death, never to be displayed again.

Finally, one of the greatest and most famous daredevil/escape artists of all time made an appearance in Rochester. In May 1907, Harry Houdini, accompanied by his wife and mother, performed one of his most popular stunts. From the top of the Weighlock Bridge near Court Street he jumped into the Erie Canal wearing not one, but two, pairs of handcuffs. The entire stunt was filmed for the first time using, of course, Rochester's famous Kodak film. The Union and Advertiser chronicled the event. *"Mounting to the top of the bridge truss Houdini waved his manacled wrists to the crowd, shouted 'Goodbye' and leaped. As he entered the water he burst a pair of cuffs asunder. Fifteen seconds later he reappeared with the other pair of cuffs dangling from one wrist and then sinking again he came to the surface again with the cuffs completely unfastened, waved them above his head and swam to the towpath."*

In just one hundred years of Western New York history the thrills grew bigger and bigger, and more death-defying...just to satisfy the ever-growing appetite of the crowds. To quote Molly Kirker:

> *The American dream is a belief that human ingenuity can generate endless, perhaps even extravagant possibilities.*

FROM CONSERVATION TO PRISONERS OF WAR

The test of our progress is not whether we add more to the abundance of those who have much; it is whether we provide enough for those who have too little.
(Franklin D. Roosevelt – January 20, 1937)

In the 1930s the United States was hit with a powerful blow when the stock market crashed and the country fell into a deep depression; businesses failed, and thousands of Americans found themselves out of a job and with no income. Families were ripped apart as desperate mothers and fathers abandoned their children at orphanages, or even worse, sold them so that they would be able to survive for just another month or two. The effects were felt the worst by the lower and middle classes. Luckily, Rochester was not hit as hard as other areas of the country. The banks remained open, but dividends were cut. Employers like Hickey-Freeman reduced the hours of their workers, but they all kept their jobs. And the soup and bread lines in Rochester were shorter than those in other cities.

The local governments gave as much as they could to those who needed it the most, but it was just not enough, and it was clear that the federal government needed to step in and step up. To combat the effects of the depression and pull the economy out of a deep hole, President Franklin D. Roosevelt introduced the New Deal to establish programs and laws to do just that. The main objective was the three Rs; relieve, recover, and reform. It created jobs that would relieve the poor and unemployed, which would help the economy recover. It also mandated a series of regulations that would help reform the financial system of the country to help ensure that the United States would not fall into another depression as devastating as this.

One program that provided the relief the poorest citizens needed was the Civil Conservation Corps or CCC. The main objective was to rebuild the country's infrastructure. Unemployed young men who were not married and between the age of seventeen and twenty-eight could enlist in the CCC for a six month to two year commitment. In return, they received food, housing at work camps and medical care while earning a generous wage to support their families. Each man earned $30 a month, equivalent to $570 today, of which $25 had to be sent home.

CCC Camp #1252 or the Moscow Road Camp in Hamlin opened in May 1935. It could accommodate two hundred men at a time and in the six years that it was in service, 1,600 men "camped" there. The purpose of the Moscow Road Camp was to turn a small county park into the beautiful state park that it is today. The camp enlistees built Hamlin Beach State Park with their own hands; from the lumber cut and milled on site and the stone blocks cut there as well. The pavilions, snack bars and bathrooms were constructed of Medina sandstone and locally harvested lumber. They poured the concrete for the sidewalks and breakwalls. Creating a state park that spanned 1,200 acres was a daunting task, but being able to earn a living wage to support their family was worth it. Across America thousands of young men were doing the same.

Hamlin CCC Camp before it closed

Our European allies were pulled into the Second World War and needed all types of supplies and materials. Factories that had closed due to the depression were reopened and retooled to make just about anything that would be needed on the battlefield and frontlines. They needed to be able to run seven days a week which meant lots of high-paying jobs would be available. While the CCC camps provided necessary labor for infrastructure jobs, the country had new needs for the enlistees, especially with the world at war. For that reason, the Moscow Road Camp closed in August 1941.

After the camp closed, a handful of buildings were dismantled. The rest would remain intact and ready for its next adventure...and what an adventure it would be. With all the able-bodied men either working in the factories or serving in the US military, a strain was put on the local farmers that relied on seasonal help to plant and harvest their crops. A deal was made to all the camp to be used as a housing facility for migrant workers to be hired by the farmers as field laborers. A group of Bahamians in the summer of 1943 were the last to use the camp for that purpose. Not but a few months later would it hold other foreign "visitors."

Japanese kamikaze pilots bombed Pearl Harbor, Hawaii on December 7, 1941. The United States had tried to stay out of the fight, but it seemed as if the fight came looking for us. And the unprovoked attack on American bases in the Pacific drew us in the war. For years the fighting raged on in the Pacific Theater and on the European continent. As with most wars, prisoners were taken on the battlefield by both sides of the line. The Allies kept them at detention camps all over the world. When Italy surrendered, the generals with the United States army sent their Italian prisoners back to the states, of which 110 arrived at the former Moscow Road Camp in September 1943. A month later on October 13, 1943, Benito Mussolini swore his allegiance to the Allies and all the prisoners were released and sent back to Italy.

Not long after the Italian soldiers returned home, new "guests" arrived at the camp and the welcome mat was not warmly put out for them. When the German prisoners of war arrived on June 30, 1944, everything at the camp was ready for them. Believed to be a much greater threat than their Italian counterpart, an eight-foot barbed wire fence with guard towers was erected as well as the installation of outdoor and search lights. The single cots in the barracks were replaced by bunk beds to double the camp capacity. Depending on the time of year and demand of labor, the prisoner population at the camp fluctuated. In the fall of 1945, 452 prisoners were held at the Moscow Road Camp which filled the barracks to the brim and seventeen tents had to be pitched to accommodate the overflow. Even with the prospect of sleeping outside in the cold Western New York weather, the captured German soldiers were glad to be sent to prison camps in the United States because the living conditions were better at the camps than what they endured on the front lines. At least at the camps they were guaranteed food and water, as well as protection from the elements.

Prisoners at the camps were put to work on farms and at processing plants for a small stipend, as directed by the Geneva Convention's rules. Under the constant watch of heavily armed guards, some of the prisoners were transported to work at a plant in Hilton. Children would ride their bikes to the packing plant to stand by the chain-linked fence to watch them work and listen to them talk to each other in German. The children were not afraid of them, just curious. The German prisoners would sometimes give the boys money to buy cigarettes and chocolate for them, often tipping them the change. There had been no documented reports that a prisoner caused any trouble, and the locals began to see them as human beings instead of the enemy.

The Moscow Road Camp was not the only prison camp in the area, a much smaller camp sat on Cobb's Hill in Rochester. As with the Hamlin camp, it housed Italian prisoners in September 1943 and around one hundred German prisoners in the summer of 1944. At first the residents that lived near the Cobb's Hill camp were afraid of what might happen if the prisoners escaped, but Colonel John McDowell, who oversaw the camp, advised the Rochester citizens to treat the Germans with respect and there would be no problems. Over time they even became comfortable with the camp being in their backyards and enjoyed the sound of the music drifting from the camp on the evening breeze. In August 1944, about two hundred Rochester residents clashed with the American soldiers guarding the camp. The residents had gathered in the field outside the camp to listen to the prisoners sing, the soldiers became offended when the crowd offered applause. The police needed to be called to disperse the crowds. According to an account from the *Times Union* on August 14, 1944, "*Fist fights started. Joseph Sauer and his son, Frederick, were beaten up by the soldiers...(when the police arrived at the scene) Mrs. Sauer was swinging her pocketbook at a soldier.*" People continued to gather in the field and the soldiers grew increasingly short-tempered. The city of Rochester was unsuccessful in diffusing the situation and saw they only solution was to petition the United States military to close the camp, a request that was denied though interaction between the prisoners and the city residents was banned.

There was little excitement at the Moscow Road Camp in comparison to Cobb's Hill, however there were witness accounts that a guard had gone crazy one night and fired his machine gun from the tower toward the lakeshore.

World War II came to an end on September 2, 1945, and the prisoners at both camps were eventually released. After returning home to Germany, many brought their families back to the United States and became citizens. The Moscow Road Camp closed for good in January 1946. The army dismantled all the buildings and nature reclaimed what was left. For over sixty years its history remained hidden until the Friends of Hamlin Beach State Park began to clear the site. The group has placed informative signage throughout so that visitors can take a self-guided tour.

HUMANITY OF LOST SOULS

Mental health and how to treat mental illness has always been a societal issue. How it was dealt with has evolved over time. Before the 1800s, mental illnesses were looked at as more of a curse, and in some cases, as an affliction cast upon that person by the Devil himself. Church leaders had supreme control of the congregations and would strike fear in the minds of the poor and uneducated by telling them that any deviation from God's (and the church's) laws could bring down this type of punishment on them and their family. For example, if a woman had a child out of wedlock, and the child was born with a mental illness, it was because God punished the woman for her transgressions with an "idiot" child (there was no political correctness at that time). Families hid their lunatic relatives away from their neighbors as best they could so that they would not be judged. This was especially true in small communities and remote villages. In rural areas, the insane were targets of "witch hunts," automatically blamed for various crimes and unexplained events. Therefore, instead of getting the help that they desperately needed, they were often imprisoned and tortured. In the nineteenth century, the names that were used to describe them were demeaning and cruel. Society would tolerate them but felt that they could not offer anything of value to society. Then advances in medicine toward the end of the nineteenth century shed some light on the disorders and diseases of the brain. Courses of treatments were developed, but they were horrifically painful and sometimes deadly. The scientists who made significant breakthroughs in psychology and psychotherapy did not come on the stage until the beginning of the twentieth century. Until these medical pioneers arrived, people advocated for the humane treatment of the mentally ill.

In 1824, the New York legislature passed a law that required every county across the state to open a poor or almshouse that would support those who could not take care of themselves and were a burden to society. Services at the county homes were not just limited to taking care of the poor and destitute citizens; by law, the door was open to the community's lunatics as well. While the mentally ill were figured into the equation when the law was written, the legislation had no idea about the true extent of the problem. To say that there was an increase in the number of mental illness cases would be incorrect. It would be more accurate to say that the extent of the problem was brought to light.

Within twenty years after the first poorhouse opened in the state, so many people who suffered from mental illness turned to the county for help that the state was compelled to open a hospital dedicated to only those cases. In 1843, the New York State Asylum at Utica opened, followed by several private mental institutions. Although the Utica Asylum was equipped to handle most cases, there were limitations to the care that it provided. Only acute cases were admitted, and if patients were not "cured" within two years, they were remanded back to the custody of their county home as a lost cause. Those deemed incurable or "chronically" insane by their physicians would not even be seen at the state asylum at all. Most families could not afford the small fortune to have them privately institutionalized; as a result, they remained in the care of the poor house. In the meantime, the state asylum quickly filled and became overcrowded. The protocols carefully set pertaining to the treatment of patients were soon disregarded. Patients were discharged before their two years were up regardless of the progress in their recovery to accommodate new patients in desperate need of help as well. The system broke down quickly and people seeking treatment were turned away.

The insane were once again forced to turn to their local poorhouses. The dilemma facing the poorhouses was that they were not equipped to handle any type of mentally ill resident, especially those whose conditions were chronic and deemed incurable. Physicians at them generally had their own private practice in addition to their duties at the county home. The doctors made regular rounds to see the residents once a month unless there was an emergency. And even then, they had limited education regarding mental disease. General everyday care was routinely maintained by stewards and matrons, the equivalent to a hospital orderly today. It was no stretch of the imagination that the treatment of the insane was less than stellar. In fact, they were often "chained and shackled to the floors and walls in windowless basements, outhouses and sheds."

Sylvester D. Willard, a physician from Albany, was appalled by the mental health system, and in the 1860s, he played an important role in reforming the treatment of the mentally ill. He came from a long line of humanitarians, religious leaders and doctors. Therefore, Dr. Willard took his duty to serve his fellow man seriously. His integrity and morals are summed up perfectly in this excerpt from his 1864 obituary. *"He possessed a large executive ability and power to readily bringing other minds into harmony with his own...His moral qualities were akin to his intellectual one. He had great simplicity and directness of character. With him the question 'What is right?' was all absorbing and he sought to settle it by light from about and within."*

Willard's Grandview

Dr. Willard oversaw the investigation into each poorhouse in New York State and was astounded by what he found. It was much worse than he could have ever anticipated. Cleanliness was not enforced; the mentally ill residents were covered in their own filth and feces. Many slept on loose straw spread directly on the hard floor. The straw was wet with urine and feces, not unlike the pens that housed livestock in a barn, and it appeared to have not been changed in days even weeks. There was inadequate ventilation, which meant that they had little or no fresh air. Some of the residents were kept in dark, cramped cells or cages, often with no shoes and clothing, which became extremely unbearable in the winter months. He took his findings to the New York State legislature to campaign for change. Six days before his death, a law was passed that called for a new state asylum, which would be named after him. This was the answer to everyone's prayers, or so they thought.

Willard Asylum for the Insane started off small, a 250-bed facility in the old agricultural college building on the eastern shore of Seneca Lake. The open landscape and farmland was the perfect location. It would provide hope for those who had become hopeless.

The very first patient at the asylum arrived at Ovid Landing by steamboat on October 12, 1869. Mary Rote, a twenty-eight-year-old Columbia County woman, has been a resident at the poorhouse there for more than a decade. The exact nature of her illness has never been revealed; however, the treatment that she received there and her physical appearance when she arrived at the dock have been. Mary spent ten years of her life chained to the wall of her room, reportedly with no bed or clothing. When she got off the boat, she was physically deformed; her atrophied muscles made it nearly impossible for her to walk. Mary did not arrive alone. There were three men who also came across the lake, but she was given the honor of being registered as patient number one. The men arrived in no better condition than Mary. Two were bound in chains and irons, and one unfortunate soul was confined to a box no bigger than three and a half feet square, the box resembled a chicken crate.

At first, the main objective, and Dr. Willard's vision, was to transition the patients from the horrific treatment that they were used to at the county homes to the compassionate care that they should receive at the asylum, as the definition of asylum is "a place of retreat and security, a sanctuary." Each new patient was bathed, clothed and fed – cared for; a concept that was foreign to many of them. No occupational skills were taught; however, the asylum was designed to be self-sufficient. Those who had tangible skills and talents were put to work. By some accounts, there were reports of slave labor – long hours and harsh working conditions. Though, none of the accusations have ever been substantiated. Those who were unable to work were given activities like puzzles and crafts to occupy their time.

There was a dark side behind the façade. A trip to Willard often became a one-way ticket to a living hell, especially during its first seventy-five years. For most, the only way out was in a plain pine box. In fact, nearly half of the fifty-eight thousand patients treated at Willard died there. The cause of those death was not always attributed to their illnesses but rather inhumane and experimental treatments. Unfortunately, we will never know the truth, because the death records are either incomplete, missing or sealed by the state.

The stigma that the families believed to be attached to them for having a relative with a mental illness led to the abandonment of lunatics on the asylum's doorstep. Aside from being admitted for bona fide mental illnesses, people were sent to an asylum for other reasons ranging from the disturbing to the absurd; intemperance, masturbation, inbreeding, desertion by husband, novel reading, time of life, superstition, grief and laziness. Most of the time, the family was simply trying to avoid embarrassment about what were minor illnesses and behavioral problems. Because of this embarrassment, almost all the patients who were dropped off would never see their families again. Even after death, patients remained alone, their bodies unclaimed. During the nineteenth century, the government saw this neglect as a way to further medical research. Willard and other institutions were required by law to turn any unclaimed bodies over to a medical school to be used as research cadavers. After the law was discontinued, the bodies of the deceased were buried in the Willard Cemetery. And there they remained anonymous and forgotten, only to be known as an obscure number.

One man would make it his life's work to see that his fellow inmates were given the respect that they deserved in death that they had not been afforded in life. Lawrence Mocha was born in 1878 in Austria to parents of low standing. When he could find work, he learned the trade of metalworking to earn a decent wage. When he was twenty-seven, he suffered a severe head injury after being struck with a rock. The side effect of the injury, besides brain damage, was alcoholism. The excessive drinking led to loud and exciting singing and whistling, which led to his first stay in an asylum in Dusseldorf,

Germany. When he was released, he made his way to the United States.

In New York City Lawrence soon found employment as a window washer at Bellevue Hospital. Desperate to fit into his new surroundings, he took night classes to learn English. While working at Bellevue, he was put in an asylum for the second, and last, time. Lawrence had a "spell" in 1916; he began to sing loudly and energetically while he prayed and claimed to hear God speaking to him. The behavior quickly earned him a reservation in the psych ward, where he continued to insist that he had heard God and saw the angels.

Lawrence Mocha

At the age of forty, he was transferred from Bellevue to Willard. For the first year, he kept to himself. He began to work outside doing maintenance on the grounds, which transitioned to digging graves. He dug perfect burial plots by hand for the deceased.

For forty-nine years, he the graves of his fellow patients, unpaid. And in 1968, when he was in ninety years old, he died and was buried among the rest. Willard's ground keeper Gunter Minges said of Lawrence - "He dug until he died." During his fifty years at Willard Asylum, Lawrence Mocha dug more than 1,500 graves.

Although he worked tirelessly to give the deceased the dignity in the burial they deserved, he did not receive the same. His passing earned him a simple numbered stake. In 2015, a group working to give the recognition they deserved honored Lawrence with a plaque on a stone at his burial plot. The plaque reads:

Lawrence Mocha
June 23, 1878 – October 26, 1968
"The Grave Digger"

In his half century as a Willard patient,
Lawrence dug over 1,500 graves for his
fellow patients, who are buried
in this cemetery, that they might
have a final resting place, long
after the world had forgotten them.

The Willard Cemetery is on a hill along the eastern shore of Seneca Lake overlooking Ovid Landing. The view is picturesque and serene, a contradiction of its purpose. The only indication that there is a cemetery in the clearing comes from a sign by the road at the bottom of the hill, "Willard Cemetery – This cemetery was used from 1870-2000. Here laid to rest are 5,776 departed Willard patients."

In the northwest corner, under the canopy of hardwood trees, are the graves of thirty-eight Civil War veterans, marked and decorated with American flags. Each of the veterans served in the Grand Army of the Republic and were all patients at Willard. The southwest corner has a fenced-in area with a simple arch bearing the words "Old Jewish Cemetery." Placed in front of the arch is a large stone with "In remembrance of the Jewish residents buried at Willard Psychiatric Center 1870-1992."

The rest of the meadow holds the remains of thousands of people who died over 130 years. Originally, each grave was marked with either a wooden stake or a metal disc with their number on it. Over time the wood rotted away, the discs sank into the earth and grass covered them. To a stranger, this would appear to be a beautiful, quiet meadow.

Not all of those who died at Willard are laid to rest on the great meadow. Patients who passed away in the asylum's first few years were placed in an unmarked cemetery behind Grandview. Some were buried in "patients' row" in Ovid Union Cemetery and in unmarked graves in the Holy Cross Cemetery. In May 2016, the board of the Holy Cross Cemetery dedicated a granite monument with the names of the 268 patients buried there. Those who had not been given their due respect were forgotten after they left this earthly realm as if they had never existed. However, the stories of over 400 people were about to be rediscovered.

In 1995, New York State decided to shut Willard down. What few patients remained in the psychiatric center's care were transferred out to nursing homes and other facilities. As the last patients were discharged, the staff began the daunting task of cataloguing the contents of each building. A couple of workers thought they had finished the building they were assigned. As they made a final walk-through, they found a door to the attic that had never been noticed before. When the door was opened, they saw shelves up on shelves filled with suitcases and boxes. Beverly Cartwright, who was one of the first to set eyes on this treasure trove of history, said that she felt an energy in the large room the moment she opened the door and thought, "It was like they were still tied to the few remaining treasures and did not find their way home."

The attic contained 427 suitcases, neatly placed on shelves in alphabetical order and separated by gender. Each was tagged with the owner's name and patient number; they belonged to patients admitted between 1910 and 1960. They contained bits and pieces of their personal lives – things that were important to them – records, sewing notions, travel souvenirs, family photographs and letters, figurines, books and personal care items. The suitcases sat until their owners were to leave the asylum; however, no one ever left Willard. When patients passed away, their possessions, just as their bodies, were rarely claimed by the family. The staff who had developed caring relationships with them could not bear to throw them away. As time went on, the nurses and orderlies came and went, and the existence of the suitcases became forgotten, until that day in 1995. Each suitcase and box had a story to tell. Two of those stories were of Margaret and Dmytre.

Margaret was a tuberculosis nurse who suffered from the horrible disease herself. She was forcibly admitted to Willard on the simple charge that she annoyed people. She came to Willard in 1941 feeling "like a fly in a spider web," and she stayed trapped in the web for thirty-two years until her death. Margaret brought with her a staggering eighteen suitcases and boxes containing her entire life.

Dmytre and his wife come to the United States in 1949 from the Ukraine after being interred in a Nazi concentration camp during World War II. When they arrived in America, they settled in Syracuse in a largely Ukrainian neighborhood. Sophia was pregnant, and soon after moving, she suffered a miscarriage and died. Dmytre lost his mind and became delusional. He began having fantasies about being married to President Truman's daughter, Margaret. In 1952, he took a trip to Washington, D.C. and knocked on the door of the White House demanding to see his wife. He was quickly arrested by the Sevret Service and placed in a mental institution. A year later, he was transferred to Willard. Dmytre was a model patient and a prolific artist; many of his paintings are in local galleries and museums. He was one of the few who left Willard, placed in the care of a county home. He died in 2000. His suitcase remained with the others.

THE LAST OF THE 1ST NY DRAGOONS

After the first shots of the Civil War were fired on Fort Sumter, President Abraham Lincoln called for 75,000 volunteers to serve for ninety days in the Union Army as both sides believed that the conflict would be quickly resolved. We know now that the loss of American life exceeded that number nearly nine-fold by the time the war ended four years later. Training camps popped up all over New York state to prepare the men for the battlefield, most of them barely old enough to shave let alone grasp the consequences of war. In spring 1862 construction of Camp Portage began at Portage Station, now part of Letchworth State Park. The 14-acre parcel owned by Colonel George Williams had more than enough space for ten barracks, two mess halls, and officers' headquarters and parade grounds.

The first group of men under the command of the 1st NY Dragoons, as part of the 130th NY Volunteer Infantry, arrived on July 23, 1862. Their wives, sweethearts and families spent their days picnicking by the parade grounds to watch them train. For some this would turn out to be the last time they would see each other. The 1st Dragoons trained just six weeks before being sent into the fray. Only one other group trained at Camp Portage: the 136th NY Volunteer Infantry from September-October 1862. After they "shipped out," the camp closed.

In August 1903 a stone monument was erected by the survivors and family of the 1st NY Dragoons. It is engraved with some incredible facts about the regiment. There were 1,414 members in the Dragoons, of which 461 were killed or wounded; 131 died of disease, 33 died in Confederate prison camps, and 130 were killed at or died of the wounds they received at Todd's Tavern in Virginia on May 7, 1864 - the heaviest loss of any cavalry regiments in any single battle during the war. The Dragoons participated in 65 battles, engagements and skirmishes, during which they captured 1,533 prisoners, 19 pieces of artillery and 4 battle flags. As impressive as these numbers are, and as brave as the men were, we must remember that it came with a cost; almost one out of every five men from the Dragoons did not return home to their loved ones.

The men of the 1st NY Dragoons who did make it home, met every summer on the old parade grounds for a reunion picnic. Each year the number of men in attendance got smaller and smaller. By 1938 only a few remained, one of whom was Charles T. Peck.

Charles was 22 years old when he answered Lincoln's call to join the Union Army to fight on distant battlefields to preserve this country. He quickly moved up to the rank of second lieutenant, bravely fighting until he fell ill to a month-long illness and fever which caused him to be medically discharged in 1863. Charles chose to move to Rochester and attend Eastman Commercial College in Reynolds Arcade. He used his business training to expand his father's shoemaking business to have offices in Elmira, New Jersey, Philadelphia and Rochester. Until his death, he called Rochester home.

Charles was proud of his service and was an active member of the Grand Army of the Republic. During his time with the 1st NY Dragoons, he created an unbreakable bond with his regiment and never missed a reunion. The August 25, 1938 edition of the Rochester Democrat and Chronicle ran the following article about his attendance at the reunion.

Lone Veteran to Carry-on Tradition

When 98-year-old Lieutenant Charles T. Peck sets foot on the old Portageville drill grounds in Letchworth Park today a tradition that dates to the Civil War days will be single-handedly carried on.

The First New York Dragoons will be represented by only one member at the 69th annual reunion of the fighting unit, but the shadowy ghosts of the 1,414 young me who trained for service there in 1862 will be marching at Lieutenant Peck's side – in his memory at least – this afternoon.

Only three of the regiment are still living, the Rochester man said as he prepared to make the trip. He said he will be the only one of the three to appear on the old drill grounds.

During the last 68 years Lieutenant Peck, of Monroe County's few surviving veterans of the war between the Blue and Gray, has not failed to attend a single reunion 'so far as I can remember.' It's been a long way back – 68 years – and he 'may have missed just one get-together; I'm not sure.'

Lieutenant Charles T. Peck joined the marching ghosts on the parade grounds when he passed away at the age of 99 on August 12, 1939, just days before the 70th annual reunion. The following year, instead of a reunion, a memorial service was held to honor the 1,414 deceased service men.

Charles T. Peck

LINCOLN'S VISITS TO ROCHESTER

Near this spot on the morning of
February 18, 1861
Abraham Lincoln addressed the
citizens of Rochester

This sentiment is engraved on a plaque bolted to the stone wall along the Inner Loop to commemorate the first of two visits Lincoln made to the Flour City.

Abraham Lincoln was elected to the highest office in the land, President of the United States on November 6, 1860, at a time when the nation was in great turmoil. Just months later, his journey to Washington, D.C., his new home, began. Lincoln boarded the train in Springfield, Illinois for his March 4th inauguration on February 11, 1861. During the 12-day trip, he made 101 stops, including one in Rochester.

15,000 people waited by the tracks near the New York Central depot to greet their new commander in chief. At the time the train tracks had not yet been raised, and the station was on Mill Street at the edge of the falls. The Waverly Hotel, near the depot, was covered in patriotic red, white and blue buntings and the Perkins' Silver Coronets waited for Lincoln's arrival at which time they would play "Hail to the Chief" for the Waverly's balcony. Once the train was in sight, the sound of cannons rang through the air from Falls Field across the river from the train station.

As the Presidential train slowly passed through the train station, a young boy jumped onto the rear platform of the caboose, shook Lincoln's hand, and said, "How do you do, Mr. Lincoln?" As if he was just an ordinary person.

The stop was brief, no more than six minutes, more than twice as long as it would take him to recite his famous Gettysburg Address. During the mere moments he was in Rochester, he shared these words with its citizens –

"It is a matter of welcome surprise to me to meet, at so early an hour in the morning, such a multitude of people, and I must say it is the largest assemblage I met since I started on my journey. You have not assembled to greet me merely the man, but the representative of the American people. I cannot promise to address you at length; the time allotted for my stay among you will not admit it. If I should make extended remarks at every place where my fellow citizens had and are to assemble to see me, I should not reach the Capitol in time for the inauguration. It is a great gratification to me to see you, and I heartily thank you for your kindness."

The first shots of the American Civil War were fired upon the Union soldiers at Fort Sumter on April 12, 1861 in Charleston, South Carolina by troops of the South Carolina militia. Hundreds of men and boys from Rochester answered Lincoln's call to arms to defend the Union. For four years the country was being ripped apart while one man tried to keep it together. At the end of the horrific war, almost 900,000 lay dead and hundreds of thousands were wounded, Lincoln thought that the worst was over. He was so wrong, and it was this mistake in judgment that would bring him to Rochester a second time.

Lincoln, feeling a little lighter in spirit, decided to escort his wife Mary Todd Lincoln to Ford's Theatre on April 14, 1865 to see the play *Our American Cousin* starring a dashing John Wilkes Booth. Booth was a Southern sympathizer who had been plotting with six other men to kidnap Lincoln, the Vice President and Secretary of State. Booth knew the President was going to attend the play that night and waited until the right moment to put his plan into action and take the fate of the South into his hands. He snuck up to the Presidential box and scuffled with the guard outside the door. After he had the guard incapacitated, Booth burst through the door and shot Lincoln in the back of the head with a derringer that he carried in his breast pocket. After the deed was done, Booth jumped from the box to the stage below. His escape from the theater would result in an eleven-day manhunt which ended with John Wilkes Booth dead in a Virginia tobacco barn by a bullet from the gun of Sergeant Boston Corbett.

Back to the events at Ford's Theatre. While Booth fled the crime scene, President Lincoln clung to life and Mary screamed for help as she cradled his slumping body. The White House was too far for him to be transported in his condition, so a group of soldiers carried their Commander in Chief from the theater to the home of a tailor across the street. Doctors were called to the residence to try and save the life of the 16th President, but they knew that the wound he suffered was mortal and that no more could be done. At 7:22am on April 15, 1865, Abraham Lincoln breathed his last breath.

As news of Lincoln's assassination reached the American people, the country fell into a deep mourning. It was decided that he would be laid to rest at Oak Ridge Cemetery near his home in Springfield. His coffin was loaded onto a nine-car funeral train on April 21st to begin the thirteen-day journey home to eternity.

Lincoln's funeral train

Abraham Lincoln's funeral train arrived in Rochester at 3:20am on April 27, 1865. When the train approached the station, a military salute was fired from the Andrews Street Bridge. As the train sat at the Rochester station for fifteen minutes, the sorrow-filled residents removed their hats while a band played a funeral dirge. Then the long black train pulled away.

ONTARIO COUNTY COURTHOUSE

It took eight hard fought, bloody years for the colonists to win their independence from the British government during the American Revolution. Victory allowed them to forge a path into the vast wilderness, a new frontier. Even though the "Red Coats" had been defeated, the woods were not yet safe from the enemy. Before the, now citizens of a new country, could go west General George Washington sent Major General John Sullivan and his troops to clear them of renegade Indians that had sided with the British armies and massacred innocent settlers in the name of the crown. Washington wanted to not only make sure the "western" frontier was safe for the expanding nation, but he also needed to make a statement that the Americans were a force to be reckoned with.

The town of Canandaigua was founded in 1788 and then a year later, the county of Ontario. Even though the frontier had been made safe from the native Americans, within the settlements, a system of law and order needed to be set. The first of three courthouses in Ontario were constructed on the town square in Canandaigua. Later that year, one of the most important events in early New York State history took place.

On a chilly November day, the Pickering Treaty, or the Treaty of Canandaigua, was signed. It would guarantee peace between the six Iroquois Nations and the young United States government. At the signing, the Iroquois were represented by Corn Planter, Handsome Lake, Little Beard, and Red Jacket. Two months after the treaty was signed in Canandaigua, President George Washington made it official with his signature. 228 years later, the Treaty of Canandaigua remains active. The history making day was commemorated with a rock on the square.

Lawlessness in the 1790s was different than it is today. The first jury trial west of Albany was held in the Ontario County courthouse, a serious crime at the time...the theft of a cowbell. Not all the cases heard in the early days were so trivial. Around the turn of the 1800s, a case that could have ignited a powder keg was tried in front of a judge and jury. Stiff-Armed George was accused of killing John

Hewitt on the front porch of his log cabin. George was a Seneca Indian and John was a settler. Stiff-Armed George needed a good defense, and the great orator Red Jacket took on the case. The evidence was so great against George that not even Red Jacket's smooth talking could sway the jury to find him not guilty. The sentence of death by hanging was handed down in April 1803, though the punishment would never be carried out. Even though there was a treaty of peace, peace was hugging a thin line. Governor Dewitt Clinton feared tribal protests and riots and pardoned George nine years later. The pardon had strings attached to it. In exchange for his life, George had to leave New York State for good. Stiff Armed-George lived out his life on the Allegheny Reservation in Pennsylvania.

This country was built on freedom, including religious freedom. Though it was supported by the Constitution, many did not accept it. A perfect example was the trial of Jemima Wilkinson. Jemima was born into a strict Quaker family in 1759. A severe illness left her bedridden and on death's door. Prospects for recovery were bleak. Her recovery was a miraculous one, after which she would introduce herself as the vessel for Jesus Christ, God, and the Holy Ghost. People believed that she had lost her mind. Jemima also denounced her old identity and started her own religion and became a "Publick Universal Friend." Her neighbors treated her as an outcast and Jemima thought that if she moved to Penn Yan she could start over and practice her faith with no prejudice. She was wrong.

James Parker, a "friend" of Jemima, fought with and soon became one of her biggest adversaries. He brought the charge of blasphemy against her four times. She was able to escape trial the first three, but with the fourth, she found herself in the Ontario Courthouse in front of Judge Ambrose Spencer. After a quick trial and a not-guilty verdict, Judge Spencer asked Jemima Wilkinson to address the courtroom with a sermon. When she finished her speech, the judge gave the following remarks to those in the gallery. "We have heard good counsel and if we live in harmony and do what this woman has told us, we shall be sure to be good people and reach a final rest in Heaven."

Just thirty years after the courthouse was built, a new one was constructed to replace it. The first one wasn't demolished right away but was renamed the Star Building and served as a courthouse, post office and storehouse until it was finally torn down in 1899.

The second great hall of justice was built in 1824. It would witness one of the biggest scandals of the early 19th century, known as the "Morgan Affair." William Morgan did not have an easy life to say the least and it was about to get worse. When he was 45 years old, he took 16-year-old Lucinda as his bride. Three years after the wedding, Morgan moved his family to Canada to open a brewery. It was a risky move, especially since he had absolutely no experience in the business. Though it wasn't Morgan's inexperience that closed the brewery's doors, it was a fire that destroyed it and his dreams of success. Within two years, they returned to the United States and settled in Batavia, NY to begin a new chapter in his life.

William Morgan tried to join the York Rite Masonry lodge in Batavia to be a Freemason, but he was denied membership. However, the old saying goes "when one door closes, another one opens." In 1825, William was able to join the York Rite Lodge in LeRoy just east of Batavia. He assumed that because he was now a member of the LeRoy lodge, he would automatically be accepted in the new lodge forming in Batavia. His assumption was incorrect, and William was denied membership for a second time. He believed that he was on a blacklist and decided to seek revenge on the entire organization, not just one lodge. William Morgan worked with newspaper publisher David Miller to write an expose that would reveal all the secrets of the Freemasons. A scandal of epic proportions exploded within a year.

In August 1826, charges were brought against Morgan, and he was arrested. A local tavern keeper in Batavia accused him of the theft of a cravat and tie. Local law enforcement took him to jail in Canandaigua. Miller paid the fine and Morgan was set free. However, as soon as he was released, he was arrested again. The charge this time was a debt of three dollars. Today debt impacts your credit score and keeps you from getting things that you want. But in the early 1800s, unpaid debt was a serious crime. Morgan was sentenced to debtor's prison and had to remain there until his debt was paid in full. Miller didn't come to Morgan's rescue this time. Another man who was said to be a "friend," though most likely a Mason, paid Morgan's debt and he was released from the Ontario County Jail. Morgan and his "friend" walked to a carriage that waited in front of the jail for them. He would be seen alive just one more time, at Fort Niagara on the shores of Lake Ontario near Lewiston.

Most people then, and now, believe that William Morgan was murdered by a group of Freemasons as punishment for his betrayal. There are a few that thought he fled to Canada to start a new life. A month after Morgan was released from jail, a body washed up on shore near the fort. It was badly decomposed, which made a positive identification possible. Two grieving widows, including Lucinda Morgan, claimed the body to be that of their missing husband. The mystery surrounding the disappearance of William Morgan has never been solved.

The courthouse/jail where William Morgan spent his last days was converted into the town and city offices for Canandaigua in the mid-1800s. The third and final courthouse to be built on the square was constructed in 1858. The most notable cases and heart-wrenching scenes happened in this building. Susan B. Anthony's trial and the only two murder trials that ended in execution were held there.

Susan B. Anthony was one of the most famous and vocal figures in the women's suffrage movement. Her outspokenness and tenacity made her a thorn in the side of many of her adversaries. Anthony and sixteen other women illegally voted in the 1872 presidential election. However, only Anthony was charged and made an example. Also charged, were the election officials that allowed the women to vote. Susan B. Anthony walked away with just a fine, but the election officials were fined and imprisoned. Anthony's supporters sent money to help paid for her legal fees. Those donations not only paid her fines and legal bill, but she used the rest of the money to pay the legal fees of the officials as well. Even after her arrest and trial, Anthony continued to fight for the right for women to vote. Fourteen years after her death, the hard-fought battle was won when the 19th Amendment was passed in 1920.

The Finger Lakes region of Western New York played a huge role in the abolition movement with "Underground Railroad" stations dotting the countryside all the way to the shores of Lake Ontario, "Station Masters" worked under the cloak of darkness to move runaway slaves closer to the freedom they sought in Canada. Hundreds, if not thousands, of the railroad's "passengers" made it to freedom, however the "train" was derailed for a few. The courtrooms of the county courthouse in Canandaigua felt the lasting imprint of emotions when run-away slaves were returned to their furious owners.

With a combined history of nearly 230 years that were filled with both tragic and celebratory events, it is no surprise that some spirits may be hanging around the city square today. Red Jacket's apparition has been seen wandering the lawn in front of the courthouse, obviously unhappy with the two losses he had suffered there: the loss of his native lands and the case of Stiff-Armed George. Inside the courthouse, the spirits run rampant. Workers refuse to work in the third-floor jury room for the simple reason that it is "creepy." One judge can agree with that assessment after he saw a blue mist change into human form and then disappear right before his eyes.

ROCHESTER ORPHANAGE FIRE

The definition of an orphan asylum, or orphanage, is residential institution devoted to the care of orphans - children who's biological parents are deceased or otherwise unable or unwilling to take care of them - Wikipedia

When the almshouses opened across New York state in 1825, adults and children were provided with housing and care. The children were forced to work instead of being educated and were vulnerable to deviants that also called the county poor houses home. A group of Protestant women felt that the children needed a safer place of refuge, and the Female Association for the Relief of Orphan and Destitute Children was formed. They opened a home on South Sophia Street, present day Plymouth Avenue, in 1837 with nine children to care for. By the end of the first year that number grew to fifty-eight and they were forced to find larger accommodations. The association raised money with the help of the community was able to build a larger and more modern institution on Hubbell Park, which became the Rochester Orphan Asylum.

Many situations brought children to the asylum. The most obvious reason was that both parents were deceased. But they were often brought to an orphan asylum if one parent was seriously ill, had a widower father that could not or would not care for them, or the family in dire straits financially. Nearly 3 out of the five children under the care of the Rochester Orphan Asylum had at least one living parent. In those cases, the parents and/or grandparents were required to pay \$1.50 a week to stay there, which helped cover the cost of the room and board, food and medical expenses. By the end of the 19th century, the Rochester Orphan Asylum cared for one hundred and nine children, and it was one of four such institutions in the city. Imagine how many children were cared for altogether.

One of the worst tragedies in Rochester's history happened on January 8, 1901 at the Rochester Orphan Asylum. A tragedy which would leave 30 people dead and scores of others scarred for a lifetime.

Neither Mr. Erhardt, the custodian, nor the rest of the staff was aware that the gas jet for the steam iron in the laundry room had been left open. For hours natural gas filled the room and eventually began to seep out under the door. Around eight o'clock, after the children had settled into bed for the night, the staff began to close the building. When the eleven o'clock rounds were made, Sarah Ashdown thought that she detected the faint odor of gas but ignored it. Martha Gillis, who oversaw the boys' dormitory, locked the door between it and the rest of the orphanage...as she did every night. The actions of both women would prove to be fatal.

Gas filled the hallway and was ignited by one of the gaslights. Mr. Erhardt got the alarm and was at the orphanage within a minute, only to find that the fire had burned itself out. Moments later an explosion rocked the boiler room in the basement with such for that it sent a plume of gas into the conservatory in the first floor. Two men walking down Plymouth Avenue felt the concussion from the explosion and when they saw the smoke, they activated the fire box at the corner.

The explosion erupted into monstrous flames and thick smoke caused screaming and panic throughout the building. The children and staff frantically looked for a way out. Some had made it to the roof but were not near the fire escapes. The rutted muddy street began to freeze, which made it difficult for the firemen to get to the asylum and caused one horse-drawn rig to overturn. It took them over half an hour to reach the blaze, and by then the west wing of the building was almost completely engulfed by the raging inferno and had begun to spread to the rest of the building. Many of the windows in the building would not open, which was a horrific scene for the bystanders in the street who stared up at the soot covered faces of children as young as two pressed against the glass, screaming for help.

Children emerged from the smoke and ran to the blanket filled arms of neighbors that took them into their homes for the night. Firemen carried unconscious children from the building, many of whom died in the arms. It was said that "even the firemen, accustomed to such fire scenes, could in some instances scarcely refrain from tears."

The *Democrat and Chronicle* reported; "*A woman screamed that more children were still on the second and third floor; firemen, policemen and citizens hurried up and came back down with four or five children, all of who were unconscious. They were taken across the street where some of them died. Others died on the way to the hospital.*" An unknown newspaper informed their readers the following day; "*Soon after the flames burst forth, white figures could be seen frantically rushing from room to room, faced peering from the windows seeking some means of escape from the terrific heat and strangling smoke. Some fainted in plain sight of the heroically working firemen.*"

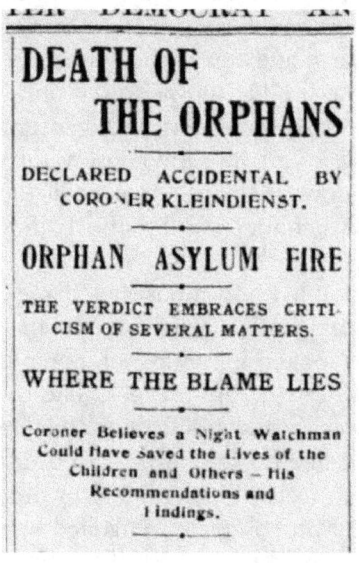

As the sun rose that morning the magnitude of the destruction was laid out before them. The asylum was in complete ruins. Twenty-seven children and three of their caretakers perished that night and in the days that followed.

Most of the children who died in the fire were laid to rest at Mount Hope Cemetery in the Rochester Orphan Asylum plot. The fire caused the city to reevaluate the antiquated fire codes and stricter laws were written and an assistant fire marshal was hired to enforce them.

ROCHESTER RIPPER

Dear Boss,

I keep on hearing the police have caught me but them wont fix me just yet. I have laughed when they look so clever and talk about being on the right track. That joke about Leather Apron gave me real fits. I am down on whores and I shant quit ripping them till I do get buckled. Grand work the last job was. I gave the lady no time to squeal.

How can they catch me now. I love my work and want to start again. You will soon hear of me with my funny little games. I saved some of the proper red stuff in a ginger beer bottle over the last job to write with but it went thick like glue and I cant use it. Red ink is fit enough I hope haha. The next job I do I shall clip the ladys ear off and sent to the police officers just for jolly wouldn't you. Keep this letter back till I do a bit more work, then give it out straight.

My knife's so nice and sharp I want to get to work right away if I get a chance.

Good luck.

Yours truly

Jack the Ripper

Don't mind me giving the trade name. Wasn't good enough to post this before I got all the red ink off my hands curse it no luck yet. They say Im a doctor now. Haha.

The Whitechapel neighborhood in the east end of London was rocked by the brutal killings of five women, known prostitutes, for three months in the fall 1888. On August 31st, Jack claimed his first victim, Mary Nichols. And his final murder on November 9, 1888 was of Mary Jane Kelly who was so brutally attacked that when her body was discovered it was nearly impossible to identify the remains as human. Jack the Ripper is still one of the most infamous serial killers and the murders to this day remain unsolved. The detectives had little to go on and without the advances in forensic science today, what evidence they did have was useless. They were able to determine that the killer had a deep hatred of women due to the vicious nature of the killings; each woman's throat was slashed, and she was disemboweled. He (or she) had a medical or surgical backgrounds because the victims' female organs were removed with impeccable skill and taken as a souvenir. And then there were the letters. During the killing spree, the murderer sent letters to Scotland Yard boasting about the "good job" he did with each woman, almost taunting them. The beginning of this chapter starts with one of the letter Jack the Ripper sent. Although London saw similar killings until 1891, they were deemed to be copycats and only the first five are linked together with the certainty that they were the work of the same hand. There was a long list of possible suspects that ranged all classes of citizens, including members of the Royal family. Two Americans were also on the list; HH Holmes, America's first serial killer, and a gentleman from Rochester, New York.

Francis Tumblety was an Irish immigrant who came to America in 1836 and settled in Rochester with his parents and ten siblings. Even when he was a young man, Francis had established a reputation of a troublemaker with local law enforcement. At the age of seventeen he was arrested for selling pornographic books along the Erie Canal from Rochester to Buffalo. Tumblety later gained more respectable employment as a janitor at Lispenard Hospital at 19 Exchange Street, which specialized in "gynecological operations and 'cures' for sexual temptations." This is most likely where Tumblety's perversions started, each of the jobs he had up until this point shows a connection to women in a sexual context. But how do we know for shore that he had a perversion to women? It is no secret that he hated women, and he has a strong disdain for prostitutes because he had a failed marriage to one. Tumblety left Rochester and moved around a lot, never staying in place for more than several months at a time. During a search of a home he occupied in Washington, DC in 1881 or 1882, an extensive and disturbing collection of uteruses and other female reproductive organs preserved in jars was found which he probably acquired in Detroit, Michigan or Canada where he had set up shop as a "great physician. It is important to note that there is no record the Francis Tumblety attended medical school. He was nothing more than an Indian herb doctor, snake oil salesman and a practitioner of quack medicine.

In the late summer/fall of 1888, Tumblety was in London. It was one of many European tours that he had taken. During the Ripper killings, Francis stayed in a Whitechapel boarding house. Tumblety's movements attracted the attention of police, and he was arrested for performing "homosexual acts." They charged him with gross indecency, which was a serious offense, and held him in custody until he made bail. When Scotland Yard finally had the opportunity to question Tumblety, they determined that he could be Jack the Ripper, but they lacked the evidence to hold him. Bail was set and Tumblety was ordered to stay in London until his trial date for the indecency charges could be set. But he knew that his days of freedom were numbered and he fled England the first chance that he had. Under the assumed name of Frank Townsend, he boarded a ship to France and then to New York.

Francis Tumblety's reputation preceded him and the police department in New York City kept him under constant surveillance. And even though his capabilities were well known, the extradition back to England was blocked because the detectives lacked enough evidence. The men from Scotland Yard left New York empty handed. If Tumblety was indeed Jack the Ripper, he got off scot-free. However, the rumors and suspicions followed him for the rest of his life and into the afterlife. Francis Tumblety died on March 28, 1903, in St. Louis, Missouri. His body was returned to Rochester, where he was laid to rest in the family plot at Holy Sepluchre Cemetery.

SENECA LAKE'S WATERY GRAVEYARD

Usually when conversations turn to lake navigation and the shipping of industry in American history, one automatically thinks of the huge freightliners that silently slip through the waters of the Great Lakes. However, we tend to forget that the world was much smaller and that a one-hundred-mile trip then was as dangerous as a one-thousand-mile trip today. The big ships of the 19th century not only sailed on the Great Lakes, but also on the Finger Lakes of New York State. And there are almost as many ships that lay on their sandy bottoms.

The Native American tribes used the lakes for travel, trade, and even war, long before the European settlers came to the North American continent. With a nautical history that has spanned centuries, it is a given that scores of vessels, large and small, have made the lakebed their final resting place. There are ships in this "graveyard" whose stories stand out among the others. The steamships *Seneca Chief* (known also as the *Geneva*) and the *Onondaga* come to mind.

About twenty years after Robert Fulton built *Clermont*, the first steamboat, the *Seneca Chief* appeared on Seneca Lake in the late 1820s. The Rumney brothers, Geneva businessmen, saw a future in Fulton's steam-powered engine and wanted to use the *Seneca Chief* to dominate steam navigation on the lake. For that period, she was a good-size boat with a ninety-foot keel, nineteen feet wide and eight feet high. The *Geneva Gazette* detailed her powerful forty horsepower engine that allowed the boat to travel at a speed of ten to twelve miles an hour and reported that a trip from Geneva to Watkins Glen at the head of the lake only took five hours, less than half the normal time. She was launched in May 1828, but her maiden voyage was not until Geneva's Independence Day celebration. The *Seneca Chief* left Geneva for Watkins Glen at eight o'clock in the morning with her crew, around 130 passengers and a band. After spending a couple hours at the "Glen," she returned to her home port about eight o'clock that night. A reporter for the local paper wrote that the *Seneca Chief* made "next door neighbors" out of those at the south end of the lake, or "that hitherto remote region."

The maiden voyage would be her only pleasure cruise, the *Seneca Chief* was built for work. An article in the *Courier* detailed her purpose. *"Immediately after the Fourth the steamboat will commence her regular trips to the head of the lake daily, Sundays excepted, leaving Geneva at 7 in the morning and returning at 7 in the evening – carrying the mail in connection with a daily line of stages to Washington City. She will touch at Dresden and Bailey Town (near Ovid) to receive and deliver passengers and take freight boats in tow.* In one documented account, she pulled into the port of Geneva with ten boats in tow that were loaded with flour, pork, whiskey, and lumber.

A year after the launch of the *Seneca Chief*, the Rumney brothers upgraded her engine compartment, added a luxury cabin and a mast so that they could take advantage of the winds that tended to grace Seneca Lake.

A winter storm in January 1832 sent the *Seneca Chief* to the bottom of the lake where she was moored. When she was raised to the surface that spring, everyone was surprised to find that the damage she suffered was minimal. Soon the *Seneca Chief* was back on the water and continued to be profitable for the Rumney brothers. In 1833, they sold her to John R. Johnston and Richard Stevens, who added thirty-five to her keel and renamed her the *Geneva*. Johnston and Stevens not only bought the *Seneca Chief*, but they also purchased all the rights steamboat navigation on Seneca Lake.

The life of an early lake steamer was relatively short and by 1847, the *Geneva* had outlived her usefulness after only 20 years on the water. Instead of letting her rot, forgotten in a boatyard, they decided to make the destruction of the *Geneva* a part of the city's Independence Day festivities. It was only fitting that since she debuted on July 4th, that she should say goodbye on the same day. The *Geneva Gazette* recapped the events of that day forty-two years later in an 1889 edition of the paper.

It was to be the grand coup of the celebration. Loaded with a supply of powder she was placed far out in the lake, and a connected with an electric battery to run her. A grand spectacle was looked for by the assembled multitude on the shore. It was estimated that ten thousand people were present lining the shore at every convenient point. The electric key was touched time and again but there was no thundering response. Failing in this a party armed with a fuse was despatched in a small boat and another attempt was made to blow her up by thus igniting the powder. This even failed to work, but the boat took fire and the disappointment of the spectators was considerably lessened by seeing the relic of the grand old steamer shoot fiery tongues towards the Heaven, illuminating the harbor and the adjacent shores...The powder had been wet in some manner and its explosive qualities thus destroyed. As it was the sight was a memorable one.

Thirteen years later the steamer *Perez H Fields,* named after the New York Assemblyman from Ontario County, was built in Geneva in 1860. She was one hundred and seventy-five feet from end to end with a paddlewheel on her side, her job was to serve as a tow boat. At the time, she was one of the largest lake steamers. During the American Civil War, the *Perez H Fields* was called to duty as a transport ship. Hundreds, maybe thousands, of Union soldiers boarded her in Geneva to cruise down to Watkins Glen, where they would then go to camp in Elmira and dispersed to battlefields across the south.

Shipbuilder Bruce Springstead was commissioned by the Seneca Lake Navigation Company to transform the *Perez H Fields* into a luxury passenger steamer in 1870. When she returned to service, she was christened the *Onondaga.* She could accommodate five hundred passengers, offering them beautiful staterooms and a dining room. The *Onondaga* was also the fastest steamer on the lakes, making to trip from Geneva to Watkins Glen in just 3 hours.

During her thirty-five years, she plied a steady course up and down the lake. But just as with other steamers, new and faster ships came along, and her route was given to one of them. The *Onondaga* was no longer the belle of the lake, and she was given jobs that a ship of her age and speed could handle. She was finally demoted to the role of quarantine ship for a travelling troupe of performers with the Joshua Simkins Opera Company that came down with smallpox in 1898. They took the whole thing in stride and performed on the deck of the ship for those who watched from shore. The *Onondaga's* final curtain call would come four months later.

Handbills were handed out and posters plastered an area of a hundred miles to advertise a spectacular event that no one should miss. The *Onondaga* was to be blown up to commemorate both the explosion of the *USS Maine* on February 15, 1898, off the coast of Cuba, which started the Spanish-American War, and the end of the war in August 1898. More than five thousand people came to the shores of Seneca Lake on September 14th. Trains from Rochester, Syracuse and Utica offered special fares to Geneva so that they could watch the *Onondaga* be destroyed in the most spectacular way. Families arrived in wagons after hours on the dusty road. People picnicked, bands played and even a hot air balloon hovered overhead. The atmosphere was that of a country fair, everyone there to celebrate the sinking of the "Pride of Seneca Lake."

The *Onondaga* was towed out eight miles south of Kashong Point. The steamer had been loaded with five hundred pounds of dynamite and three hundred pounds of powder to ensure that she went down without a fight. When the dynamite was detonated the outcome was very different from that of the *Seneca Chief.* Witnesses claimed to see a five-hundred-foot mushroom cloud erupt from the ship and pieces of splintered wood rained down from the sky. After the smoke cleared, what remained of the *Onondaga* floated on the water in flames. By morning, the steamer once called the Belle of the Lake rested on the bottom of Seneca Lake.

The *Seneca Chief* and *Onondaga* are the most famous wrecks on Seneca Lake, but they are by no means the only ones. Most of the vessels that lay on the bottom of the lake are anonymous, their identity lost over the years.

Just off the shore of Glass Factory Bay, south of Geneva, another ship was lost. Mother Nature, not man, gave the lake this prize. On March 22, 1822 a winter storm blew across the lake. The gale force winds caused the waves to become angry, and visibility disappeared. In the bay a schooner with a crew of four began to founder. The cargo of lumber and furniture shifted with the rolling waves and made the ship impossible to control. To keep from being thrown overboard, the crew lashed themselves to the mast and their cries for help carried on the wind to the shore. The townsfolk could not bear to stand by and watch them slip into a watery grave, so a few brave men climbed into a small boat and risked their lives to save those of others. The rescuers were able to bring all the sailors to safety so that they could sail another day. However, the schooner lost its battle with the storm, broke apart and sank.

When you look out over the glassy surface of Seneca Lake on a beautiful summer day, try to imagine the graveyard of bones that lay just below. And remember that for every shipwreck recorded, there are dozens more than have been lost to history.

SHE'S A BRICK HOUSE

Take a drive south on Route 21 through the rolling foothills of the Appalachian Mountains in Allegany County. At any time of the year the countryside is beautiful, but during the fall months Mother Nature takes your breath away. The air is crisp and clean and as the sun starts to sink below the horizon, the amber leaves glow as if they had been set on fire. As you reach the top of the hill just outside of Andover, what lies before you is spectacular. The white church steeples peak through the tops of the trees and welcome travelers to their sleepy town. Though the streets may be quiet today, but at one time through their history of more than two centuries, Andover was very much alive.

The subject of who founded Andover isn't cut and dry. There are two men that can be given the moniker. When Nathaniel Dike arrived in the area in 1795, there were no other settlers. He blazed a trail west after the American Revolution, others would soon follow. However, Alpheus Baker was the first to live in what would be the center of town in 1807. As the wilderness opened, towns like Andover popped up and flourished all over the Southern Tier. For over one hundred years, Andover and her citizens prospered. Besides farming, small factories and processing plants were the biggest employers in the area. Businesses on Main Street flourished until the end of the 19th century. Like most towns throughout the country, Andover fell victim to industrialization and modernization. Residents looked for employment at bigger factories and companies in surrounding cities, like Hornell and Wellsville. What once was a great center of commerce turned into a bedroom community. People spent their money where they made it, and it wasn't on Andover's shrinking Main Street. Buildings and store fronts emptied one by one, shells of their former lives.

Each town has a historic district or buildings that played a more important role in history than others. These buildings embodied the spirits of their predecessors. At 5 West Greenwood Street sits an old Victorian building that is affectionately known as The Brick.

The couple who once owned it, helped shape the history of Andover.

The backyard of The Brick is the location of the first burial ground in the town. According to history-rays-place.com, John Goodwin owned a lot on Main Street and the back portion of the property held the first cemetery in town. Today, that portion of Goodwin's original lot is part of The Brick's backyard. Only a few of the earliest interments, before 1825, were laid in that ground. The children of founding father Alpheus Baker, James Woodruff, Luther Strong and Benjamin Brookins, as well as Mr. Lyons and Mrs. Lovell found their final rest there. The graves are still buried deep, but no stones mark them. To the indiscernible eye it looks like a normal yard. What a sad way to memorialize these poor souls.

West Greenwood Street first appeared on town maps in 1856. Number 5 was owned by William and Eliza Martindale and was where their carriage shop sat. William died in 1868, and his lovely wife followed him four years later. What happened to the family business after their deaths is unknown. One can only speculate that is fell victim to one of the devastating fires that plagued the town. It took only a spark to turn a wooden building to ash and smoke. When the next owner bought number 5 in 1876, it was just an empty lot. The building that would occupy that lot would have a vibrant and important history that is all but forgotten today.

Dr. William Crandall joined the medical practice of Dr. John Harmon when he came to Andover in 1858. After Dr. Harmon retired, Crandall took the practice over. Sometime in 1876, Crandall acquired the property that was once owned by William and Eliza, and he began building his grand home. Before he could move in, the house was destroyed by fire. All the accounts of the fire and its investigation pointed to the cause being of "incendiary in origin," which meant that it was criminally set. Either it was ignited by someone with a personal vendetta against Dr. Crandall or Crandall started himself because of financial problems. There are rumors that support both theories. Regardless of the cause, Dr. Crandall was able to pick up the pieces and build the beautiful three-story brick building that stands today.

Crandall was not only far more educated than most small-town doctors, he was also quite the humanitarian. He would give the best of care to anyone that walked into his office and rarely charged the poorest of his patients for his services. Dr. William W. Crandall died in Wellsville on March 19, 1899, and was buried in Alfred Rural Cemetery.

After Crandall's death, Daniel B. Spaulding purchased The Brick for his home. The Spaulding family lived in New Marlboro, Massachusetts when Daniel was born in 1820. Both he and his father were farmers, until Daniel married Phebe Barton and moved to New Hudson, New York in Allegany County to find work in the lumber industry. He worked as many jobs as he needed to provide for his family. When they arrived in Andover in 1867, Daniel gave up hard physical labor and tried his hand at running his own business. He would become a successful druggist in the town, though they only owned The Brick for a year.

The Egglestons, the next owners, gave the building life and purpose. It is under their ownership that it returned to the role of serving the community as a sanitarium and maternity home.

Hattie Borden was born on December 13, 1872, in Norwich, Connecticut. She was a sickly child that suffered from an ailment that left her paralyzed. Doctors told her family that she would never walk, but within three years of being stricken, she overcame those disabilities and proved everyone wrong. Hattie had a nurturing spirit by nature and enrolled in a New York City nursing school where she graduated first in her class. Then she met her love, Vernon Eggleston, who was only three years her senior. On

December 8, 1897 they were united in marriage and began an new adventure in Andover. Vernon had been sent to minister to the town's religious needs at the First Baptist Church, while Hattie served their medical needs when they opened the sanitarium in 1901. She truly cared for her neighbors and friends that she had made in the area. When Vernon was not preaching on Sunday morning, he managed the business of the sanitarium and joined the town druggist James Chessman in pharmaceuticals.

The world around the couple was changing, as conflicts raged in Europe and World War I broke out. President Wilson tried to keep the United States out of the war, but a series of events made the decision to remain neutral impossible and the army set foot on the battlegrounds in Europe alongside our allies in 1917. Many young men felt compelled to enlist and Vernon was no different. Through the Y.M.C.A, at the time the Young Men's Christian Association, he enlisted as a chaplain and helped carry the wounded and dead off the battlefield. He witnessed first-hand the horrors of war, while ministering to those in need of last rites and prayers while mortars and shells landed all around him. During his tour in Europe, he received a minor battle wound which he recovered from.

While her husband served his country overseas, Hattie served her community at home. When Vernon returned home, he continued to serve his fellow man as a secretary with the Y.M.C.A. He was sent to different locals all over the Western Hemisphere. Hattie was a dutiful wife, tending to things in Andover without complaint while he served thousands of miles away on the battlefield, but she missed her husband and chose to sell the sanitarium to join him on his travels across North and Central America. Vernon had been afflicted with Vasquez Disease, a rare blood and marrow cancer, while in Europe, which became complicated during their stay in California. He was confined to a sick bed with Hattie at his side caring for him. As hard as he fought to regain his health, he was unable to beat it and passed away on August 3, 1922. A heartbroken and homesick Hattie brought Vernon's ashes home to their home in the Alleghany Mountain foothills.

The following is an excerpt of the obituary published in *The Andover News* after Vernon's death.

Rev. V.L. Eggleston - Memorial services for the late Rev. V.L. Eggleston AM were held at the Baptist Church in this village,

Sunday afternoon, 3 o'clock. The church was filled with those anxious to pay respect to the memory of their departed friend. The profuse floral offerings spoke most emphatically in silent words of the love and esteem in which the deceased was held in the community. The services at the church were conducted by Rev. AD Sheppard, pastor of the church and Rev. HD Bacon, of Portville, who was pastor of the Andover Presbyterian Church for a number of years during Mr. Eggleston's radiance in this village. Mr. Bacon's remarks were in the nature of a personal tribute of a friend and brought out vividly the high character and life that had been lived in this community by the deceased.

When Hattie returned from California, she could not remain still. She resumed the work that she loved and did best. Hattie was able to buy The Brick back as a maternity home. When she was no longer able to afford the buildings upkeep, she sold it and opened the maternity home on Maple Street. Over her career, she delivered over 600 babies, without losing a single mother or child. The only thing that was able to keep her from her calling was illness. After she retired, a party was held in her honor. *The Andover News* shared the details of the joyous event with their readers.

Honors are Given to a Wonderful Woman
Celebration in Honor of Mrs. Hattie B. Eggleston's 600 Babies is Held at the Baptist Church

The May Day party was held last Saturday evening, May 5th, at the Baptist Church proved to be not only one of the most unique, but also one of the most thoroughly enjoyable events of the season.

The party, as was stated in last week's news, was in celebration of the arrival of the six hundredth baby in which Mrs. Hattie B Eggleston of this village, "Mother Eggleston" as she is lovingly known in many homes in many states, had been the nurse in attendance.

Mrs. Eggleston has welcomed babies to this old world in the states of New York, New Jersey, Pennsylvania, Colorado, California, North Dakota, Ohio and in the Panama Canal Zone, without the loss of a mother's life.

In addition to the company of 200 guests at the May Day party, Mrs. Eggleston had received over 400 telegrams and congratulatory letters from those unable to be present.

A company of 200 guests, the parents and grandparents of Mrs. Eggleston's babies, were in attendance.

Dinner was served at 5:30 and 7:00; the tables were most attractive, centered with garden flowers with dainty favors at each plate.

An excellent dinner was nicely served by a staff of young ladies, most of whom were among Mrs. Eggleston's 600 babies.

In the center of the dining room a picture of the first babe, now Mrs. Jennie McGuire Hubbard of Grand Rapids, Mich., was displayed.

Mrs. Addie Coleman and Mrs. Orris Parker were the only great-grandmothers in attendance.

The social hour passed rapidly in the pleasure of greeting numerous out of town guests, many of whom were former Andover residents.

According to Hattie Gavin, a namesake of "Mother Eggleston" and one of her 614 babies, "She was a very sweet woman. Everyone loved her. She did everything she could for anybody." Mrs. Gavin had great memories of visiting Mrs. Eggleston as a young girl. At the time of Gavin's birth, there was a blinding snowstorm raging outside and the doctor could not get through the roads, so Hattie Eggleston had to be both the nurse and the doctor, roles she had played many times.

As her age caught up with her, Hattie slowed down. A severe shoulder injury from a fall caused her arm to be amputated and she moved to Cincinnatus. A local paper published a beautiful tribute to Hattie Eggleston after her passing that read:

"Mother" Eggleston Dies in Cincinnatus - Mrs. Hattie B. Eggleston affectionately known in Andover as "Mother Eggleston," died early Friday morning, July 27, 1951, in Cincinnatus, NY., where she made her home with her niece, Mrs. Ralph Bennett since 1942. Mrs. Eggleston has been in ill health and a patient sufferer for several years.

Mrs. Eggleston was born on December 13, 1872, in Norwich, the daughter of William and Elizabeth Chapel Borden. During her childhood, she was completely paralyzed for about three years, an affliction, like many others in her life, she mastered and later graduated as a nurse from the New York City Hospital with honor of being first in her class to receive her velvet band.

December 8, 1897, she was united in marriage with Rev. Vernon L. Eggleston and came to Andover to reside, where Mr. Eggleston was pastor of the Andover Baptist Church, and has since claimed

Andover as her home, although her profession has taken her to many parts of the world. Rev. Eggleston died August 2, 1922 in California, the result of injuries received while moving wounded soldiers from the battlefields in World War I, in which he was listed in the Y.M.C.A work.

Mrs. Eggleston continued her professional work here, and about the turn of the century opened a sanitarium in what is now the Atwood Apartments on Greenwood Street (big brick house behind the bank) but was forced to give this work up because of her health. She later specialized in maternity and in her last active years operated the Eggleston Maternity Home on Maple Avenue.

Mrs. Eggleston has a remarkable record, which has been achieved by few, if any, having officiated as a nurse in charge at the births of 614 babies, and more than that, she never lost a mother and but one baby and that was the result of a prenatal condition. Her first baby was Jennie McGuire, later Mrs. Ward Hubbard of Grand Rapids, Mich., and in several instances, she officiated in second generations.

A niece, Mrs. Margery Borden Bennett of Cincinnatus, NY., who has cared for her the past nine years and two nephews, William and Emmett Ball of California, survives Mrs. Eggleston, the last of a family of ten children.

Services were held at Cincinnatus on Saturday and at the Andover Baptist Church Sunday afternoon, the Rev. Phillip French of Vestal, NY officiated the interment in Hillside Cemetery, Andover.

When Hattie could no longer afford to keep The Brick, she sold it to Edward Atwood who renovated it into apartments. During the time it was an apartment house, an incident took place that Hattie Gavin talked about during her interview as part of the documentary *Raising the Brick*. Gladys, a mentally unstable woman from Pixley Hill in Elm Valley, walked to Andover and attempted to execute a malicious plan against her sister and niece. With a butcher knife in hand, she walked into the Atwood Apartment building, climbed the grand staircase to the porch roof shouting that she wanted to kill them both. Her niece, who was just a little girl, was in school and an Andover police officer protected her until the incident was over. In the end neither were hurt and Gladys ended up at Willard Psychiatric Center.

The Brick changed hands several times, during which it became the Seaman Apartments before it sat vacant from the 1980s until around 1998. The Andover Haunted House Association purchased the property to preserve the history of the grand old lady. Through money raised as a haunted attracted at Halloween, they have been able to make some vital repairs and renovations.

In the main hallway near the grand staircase, the portraits of Vernon and Hattie hang on the wall. The floors might be dusty, and the paint is peeling, but The Brick's history is still very alive.

THE BIRTH OF MEMORIAL DAY

The Civil War was undisputedly the bloodiest war that the United States has ever been in. There were 30,000 more deaths than all the wars from the American Revolution to Afghanistan combined. What made the Civil War more tragic than the others was that it took place on American soil with brother against brother and neighbor against neighbor. For four long years, men found themselves hundreds of miles from their families and homes, fighting for a cause that did not even involve them. When the Civil War was finally over and the soldiers returned to their families, people lined the streets with flags in the air while marching bands played military stanzas. These warriors received a hero's welcome. Those who were killed in battle laid silent, buried in distant fields or their remains were returned in a freight car, greeted only by the sorrowful tears of their loved ones.

Henry C. Welles, a Waterloo druggist, believed that those who served and died for their country should be honored with the same vigor as the returning veterans were celebrated. Although the idea was a noble one, it would not come to fruition until Welles partnered with General John B. Murray, who was an officer in the 148th Regiment of the New York Volunteers. Murray was not a Waterloo native but found his way there after the war. Even though his military career was over, he continued to serve his community as the Seneca County clerk. Any veteran will tell you that you will forever be a patriot, and this was no different with General Murray who joined the local G.A.R (Grand Army of the Republic), a brotherhood of Civil War veterans who fought for the Union. Welles and Murray headed the Decoration Day committee that organized a celebration for May 5, 1866. According to the *Summary of Other Claims Regarding the Origin of Memorial Day,* it was a celebration that the entire town embraced. The publication said *"The townspeople adopted the idea wholeheartedly. Ladies of the village met at a local hall and prepared wreaths, crosses and bouquets for each veteran's grave."*

On the first Decoration Day all the businesses in town closed, all the porches and windows in Waterloo were decorated with evergreens and black buntings, while all the flags were flown at half-staff. Civic groups marched in the parade down Main Street alongside war veterans as bands played martial songs. Each grave of a fallen soldier in the three town cemeteries were adorned with wreaths and flags where services were presided over by General Murray and the local clergy. It was agreed that the celebration would take place the following year on May 6, 1867.

General George John Logan, the national commander of the Grand Army of the Republic, learned of Waterloo's Decoration Day celebration and issued G.A.R. General Order No. 11, which created a National Day of Honor for the military dead. The order read in part;

The 30th day of May 1868, is designated for the purpose of strewing with flowers otherwise decorating the graves of comrades who died in defense of their country during the late rebellion, and whose bodies now lie in almost every city, village and hamlet churchyard in the land...Let us then, at the time appointed, gather around their sacred remains and garland the passionless mounds above them with choicest flowers of springtime; let us raise above them the dear old flag they saved from dishonor...

Welles could not have been prouder to have the Decoration Day that he envisioned and helped establish become a national celebration. Four months after Logan's order, Welles passed away and left behind his patriotic legacy.

Shortly after the Civil War ended, several towns across the country held similar events, and all of them claimed to be the birthplace of Memorial Day. However, on May 26, 1966 President Lyndon B. Johnson ended the debated once and for all when he signed Proclamation 3727 – Prayer for Peace, Memorial Day which gave the honor to Waterloo.

By House Concurrent Resolution 587, the Eighty-ninth Congress has officially recognized that the patriotic tradition of observing Memorial Day began one hundred years ago in Waterloo, New York. In conformity with he request contained in the concurrent resolution, it is my privilege to call attention to the centennial observance of Memorial Day in Waterloo, New York, on May 30, 1966.

A law was signed in 1971 that made Memorial Day a federal holiday. At the time of this writing, the citizens of Waterloo celebrated this day of remembrance for 157 years.

THE DAVIS HOUSE

The Davis House, built in 1811, has been an important feature along Route 415 in Cohocton, Steuben County for over two centuries. Some say that Daniel H. Daivs built the home, while other give credit to Samuel Chamberlain. Either way Davis owned the house and farm in 1820. He was a very prominent citizen of Cohocton. Davis was the first lawyer in the village, graduating from Harvard Law School, the postmaster from 1844-1845, and a major in the local militia.

Daniel H. Davis was born on May 16, 1794, in Woodstock, Connecticut. His mother, Lydia Allen, was the sister of Ethan Allen, the founder of the Green Mountain Boys c. 1770 who during the American Revolution were instrumental in the capture of Fort Ticonderoga on May 10, 1775. Daniel married Elizabeth Van Wormer, and they had three children: Jerome, Aetna and Helen. He continued to serve his community until his death in 1870.

His daughter Helen married Hamilton Rosenkrans in 1863, and the couple raised their family in the Davis House. When Hamilton died in 1897 and Helen in 1919, they were laid to rest at the Wayland Village Cemetery.

The last member of the Davis family to live in the house was Melvin Davis Andrew, who lived there until 1920. At one time the house was used as a stagecoach stop and in the early 1900s, musical jam sessions were hosted there.

Another figure in Steuben County history had a connection with the Davis House – Joseph Rosenkrans, Jr., the uncle of Hamilton. Joseph was a prolific and famous criminal in the mid-1800s who often used the house to stash stolen goods and on occasion used it as a hideout.

Joseph's father owned a large farm where Twelve Mile Creek and the Cohocton River met in Avoca. When he died in 1837, the farm was passed down to Joseph. The Rosenkrans lived a very comfortable life. The farm was the only one in the Cohocton Valley to grow tobacco, producing over 2,000 pounds.

Though there were several criminal organizations in the Southern Tier, headed by some of the most calculating and nefarious minds, Rosenkrans was the most famous. Men usually turned to a life of crime out of necessity, however if we look at the story of the Loomis family in Waterville, it was power that fueled their lawlessness. Rosenkrans did not want for anything, he was a well-to-do farmer with plenty of land and a cash crop unique to the area for which he cornered the market. Was he in it for the power it gave him, or for the fear of him that was instilled in the people throughout the countryside?

Rosenkrans's first brush with the law was in 1840 when he was 32 years old. He and an accomplice passed a $2500 forged note in Jamestown, then days later cashed $2000 in notes in Buffalo. A banker from Buffalo who had been scammed in the deal, along with a sheriff's deputy, went to the Rosenkrans farm under the guise of having some apples pressed. Joseph smelled a rat and tried to escape, but the deputy pulled his gun and arrested him. In a Buffalo courtroom, he plead guilty to forgery in the 2nd degree. He was sentenced to five years of hard labor at Auburn State Prison.

Fires started in three Cohocton village stores on September 1, 1846, and half the business district was destroyed. Even with no witnesses or a "smoking gun," the authorities had their suspects. At the top of the list was Joseph Rosenkrans. He was arrested and indicted for arson. But after demanding a trial before a jury of his peers, the district attorney had no choice but to drop the charges. With lack of hard evidence and Rosenkrans's reputation, he would not have been able to secure a conviction. According to James D. Folts, Jr. with the Crooked Lake Review – "Even law-abiding folk admitted that Joe had some good qualities; he was a good neighbor and family man, and certainly a cleaver son of a gun. One couldn't trust him, but in a way, one couldn't help liking him."

Rosenkrans kept life in the valley interesting, especially the time he was involved in a high-speed buggy chase. By 1850, Rosenkrans had served time in prison for counterfeiting. It was a lesson he had not learned. He was indicted again by a grand jury for the same crime. Remember what I said about him being clever? When the sheriff came to take him into custody, he was gone. It took two years, and at least one failed attempt to find and capture him. Rosenkrans was driving his buggy outside of Dansville when an officer happened to be coming the other way. Officer Williams brandished his pistol and shouted, "Rosenkrans!" Did he stop and say, "How can I be of assistance officer?" No. Joseph made a U-turn and headed up the Plank Road toward Wayland. Officer Williams followed him in hot pursuit, he had those horses flying. But Rosenkrans got the best of him. He ditched his team and buggy and headed into the woods. Joseph was arrested in New York City but jumped bail and fled west. He was finally caught almost two years later in 1852 at a theatre in St. Louis. Rosenkrans was labeled in a Buffalo newspaper article as an "old and well-known counterfeiter, and the head of desperate gang whose territory encompassed three counties." He was sentenced to ten years of hard labor at Auburn. Rosenkrans, though, knew how to turn on the charm and his sentence was commuted after only two and a half years.

His final stint at Auburn State Prison came after a December 18, 1868 sentence for receiving stolen goods and grand larceny. Joseph was released in September 1870. Were his days of running a crime syndicate over? Who knows. We can only surmise that for every crime that he was convicted of, there were ten he successfully executed without punishment.

What we do know for sure is that on February 10, 1881, Joseph Rosenkrans, Jr. slipped into the annals of history as one of Western New York's greatest criminal minds.

THE LOST BOYS OF INDUSTRY

Industry, the successor of the State Industrial School in Rochester, opened in the early 1900s in Rush to house troubled boys. The boys came to Industry due to various circumstances. They could have been arrested for non-violent crimes, other disruptive behavior, or they might have been abandoned by their parents. And although it housed boys who were arrested for certain crimes, the institution was not classified as a prison or jail.

It was set up as a cottage system, with a working farm that taught the boys farming skills as well as preparing them for other skilled manual occupations. There were twenty cottages that housed twenty-five boys each. The cottages had one or two dormitories where they slept, a common living room and dining room, as well as other necessary facilities. A husband and wife also resided in the cottage as parental figures for the boys. Initially there were no locks on the doors, the boys were held on the honor system. Even though there were escape attempts at Industry, overall, the boys were content with their surroundings and sentences.

Sadly, boys who were abandoned in life were often abandoned in death as well. Unfortunately, boys would pass away at Industry and on a few occasions their remains would not be claimed by their next of kin for burial. It would then be their "second family's" responsibility to carry out the solemn duty, a circumstance too often seen at state institutions. Industry had a plot of land across the road that served as the cemetery.

Valley View Cemetery was used from 1909 to 1940 and holds the earthly remains of fourteen Industry boys. The state eventually sold a piece of land in 1993, which was unbeknownst to the new owners, including the cemetery that had fallen into an unforgiveable state of disrepair. It was not until 2014 that its condition was truly revealed. Weeds had overtaken the headstones, and the picket fences had collapsed long ago. Someone has even stolen the wrought iron entrance frame.

The first to be interred at Valley View was Wesley Ball in November 1909. The reason for the Watertown teen's incarceration in unknown and information about his death at Industry is limited as well. Wesley's death certificate lists measles as his cause of death, but Industry's doctor listed "edema of the larynx" or having choked to death in the annual report.

William Mason was also from Watertown and worked on a farm there before his trip to Industry. The date of his arrival is not known, but he spent the last 2 months of his life in the school hospital with tuberculosis, from which he died in June 1915.

Earl Wessing was abandoned by his father and held in an Utica orphanage. The troubled teen got into trouble and was deemed difficult to manage with no parental supervision. Earl bounced from the Berkshire Industrial Farm to the Industry School in 1916. Three years later he died in the 1919 flu epidemic.

Norman Young was only twelve years old when he came to Industry and thirteen when he died in the 1919 flu epidemic.

Lawrence Chenofsky arrived at Industry before 1920 and was at the institution the longest of any of the boys. On the night of September 27, 1923, three boys escaped and tried to cross the Genesee River. Chenofsky was not part of the plan that the other two boys had. "...*Two boys jumped out of a ground floor window of one of the colony houses about 6 o'clock last Thursday evening. Their escape had been carefully planned, it was learned later, but they had no knowledge of the intention of Chenofsky to follow them. The two boys swam the river and lay on the opposite bank to rest. They afterwards decided to swim back for some of their clothing left on the other bank, the lad who returned said. When they reached the bank they heard a splash in water and then everything was quiet...(Democrat and Chronicle, October 3, 1923)"* The two boys reached Buffalo and one gave himself up, was returned to Industry and told the superintendent about the splashing. A search was ordered. Five days after the escape, Larry's body was found lodged in the branches of a fallen tree.

Verne Cardinal went missing from his Carthage, New York home in September 1922 and his frantic mother called the police. When Verne was found, in his possession was a stolen Ford. His mother, Bertha, made headlines in the papers at the time of his arraignment because she had to be carried from the second floor courtroom because she had no feet. Verne was sent to Industry and Bertha to

Rochester for prosthetics. Though while she was there, just miles from her son, she failed to visit him. In October 1924, Verne died from an enlarged heart. The school's annual report had this to say about his burial: *"Verne was laid to rest in our God's Acre, a most beautiful plot set aside for the final resting places of those who have no kindred or friends to care for them when they have finished their earthly career."*

Steven Metski came from Lackawanna in Erie County. Stephen was taken to Highland Hospital in Rochester after doubling over in pain. His gangrenous appendix was removed and after a week of improved health, his died fourteen days after his admittance of an obstructed bowel on April 9, 1925. Unlike the other boys, his family wanted to bring their son's body home but could not afford it. The annual report stated, *"The father of the boy did not take the body, but he and some other relatives came to the school on April 11, when Father Predmore had the body brought to the chapel and 'Blessed the Body' and he was placed in our burial plot."*

All we know about Julius Crawford was that he suffered from tuberculosis for 6 years before he expired in March 1926. In Reverend Arthur O. Sykes wrote in his annual report *"He was buried the following day in our cemetery on the hillside as he had no parents or home. The service was most impressive and a burial such as any one could wish to have."* The other boys at the institution accompanied Julius in a respectful, paramilitary parade to his final resting place.

Wesley Brummagyn was sentenced to a year at Industry with a parole date of December 11, 1926. Four days before his release date, Wesley was admitted to the school's hospital from a illness caused by a weak heart and he was kept there until he died on Christmas Eve. He was too ill for freedom and the time passed him by.

Fifteen-year-old Vincent Celano from Buffalo, a convicted car thief and part of a theft ring, came to Industry just a week before his unsuccessful escape attempt. *"Vincent Celano, fifteen-year-old Buffalo boy, who today escaped from the State Industrial School, just outside of Rochester, attempted to make liberty certain by swimming the Genesee River and was drowned in its raging current. A farmer who heard the lad's cry for help watched him swept downstream. He had fled from a field where boys of the institution were working."* His body was found a week later and taken to the

Rochester morgue was his parents to claim. They never came and he was buried at Valley View on June 6, 1927.

Just a couple months after Frank Smith was paroled from Industry, he was working on the farm of William and Emit David. The January 25, 1930 edition of the Democrat and Chronicle reported *"Smith was fatally injured Wednesday when a tree which he was chopping down on the David Brothers farm in West Rush fell on him and crushed his chest. He had been paroled from the school last November."* Frank had no family to claim his body, so it was tenderly buried at Valley View by the inmates of the institution.

Oliver Watson was just fourteen years old when his life was cut short by tuberculosis, which he contracted from his mother just before she died. His mother had died, he had no father that he knew of, and his aunt did not want him, but he was not angry. In fact, he looked death in the face with peace. Before slipping away in the waning sunset on May 26, 1930, Oliver recited the Lord's Prayer with the chaplain at Rochester General Hospital. Two days later, he was laid to rest at Valley View with the other boys that were unclaimed before him.

Samuel Broughton was brought to Industry from Ithaca in July 1931 when he was fifteen for an unrecorded crime. When he arrived, Samuel was already suffering from chronic vascular heart disease which would take his life a year and a half later.

The last boy to be buried at Valley View was Richard Dawley from Utica. His mother died in a fire when he was five and his father disappeared, leaving him as an abandoned youth with little prospect of succeeding in life. Like Samuel, Richard had an incurable illness that took him too soon. When he was admitted to Rochester General Hospital the day before his death, he was diagnosed with kidney disease which was in the final stages. Just as the thirteen boys before him, the chaplain at Industry along with the other boys living there gave him a sendoff that every person deserved.

Valley View Cemetery has since been cleaned up and the graves of the "lost boys" wait for kind strangers to pay their respects and show that their lives mattered.

Valley View Cemetery

THE PEDDLER CAME CALLING

In the mid-1800s there was an unassuming house on Hydesville Road that had a secret just waiting to be revealed. It was rumored that unexplained events in the house had driven out family after family. The house was originally built around 1815 by Dr. Hyde (and no he did not have an alter ego named Mr. Jekyll) as a rental, many families lived there – some longer than others. For three long years the Weekmans endured the strange noises and other phenomena; figures that mysteriously appeared and icy cold touches. They packed all their belongings and left in 1846. How the family braved it for so long is unknown. The house remained empty until the Fox family moved in. It did not take them long after they moved in on December 11, 1847 to discover that the rumors were true. Each night as the family got ready for bed, a mysterious knocking was heard all around them. It seemed to come from inside the walls and continued every night for months.

The family was sure that the culprits were spirits in the house and Kate and Maggie, the youngest daughters, were determined to contact whoever or whatever disturbed their sleep. Cleverly they assigned a pattern of knocks to each letter in the alphabet, inventing an early form of morse code, to serve their purpose. After a few attempts to communicate, the entity identified itself as "Mr. Split Foot," which is another name for the Devil. The conversations with Mr. Split Foot became a regular occurrence. The developments at the Fox home began to draw the attention of their neighbors, with help from the girls who planted little seeds of curiosity in passing. It began with small groups of intrigued spectators but quickly turned into large crowds; people came nightly to watch the sisters converse with the Devil.

After a while the conversations with Mr. Split Foot ended and those with Charles Rosna began. Rosna was a 31-year-old peddler who disappeared in 1843, five years before he told his story to Kate and Maggie in March 1848. The story the ghost of Rosna told was that he came to the house to sell his goods but was murdered. He continued saying that his body was buried in the basement to hide the crime.

THE OLD FOX COTTAGE, HYDESVILLE, N. Y.
(Now Removed to Lily Dale)

From 1842-1843 the Bell family, along with their housekeeper Lucretia, lived in the house. According to an interview with Lucretia, she was home when Charles Rosna came calling. At first Mrs. Bell was not, but as Rosna showed Lucretia what he had for sale, she walked in. Something sparked a rather sinister thought in the mind of Mrs. Bell. But before she could act on that thought, Lucretia needed to be out of the picture. Mrs. Bell was fond of her, so she would not harm a hair on her head. Instead, she was called into the other room and abruptly relieved of her duties. Lucretia was upset and confused, but she quickly packed her belongings and returned to her parents' home. That was the last time she saw Charles Rosna. A few days later, Mrs. Bell called on Lucretia and offered her job back. On the way back to the Bell home, Mrs. Bell lavished her with gifts and told her all about the things she had bought from Rosna before he moved on. At the time, Lucretia had no reason to doubt her story. That night Lucretia was kept awake by rapping in the wall and at the foot of her bed. Mrs. Bell tried to explain it all away as rats in the wall. Though no amount of rat poison made the rapping stop. By the end of the year, the Bell family was gone.

The story of Kate and Maggie's otherworldly conversations reached the desks of newspapermen along the eastern seaboard.

Within a week, the country knew about the peculiar events in Hydesville. An article appeared in the April 27, 1848 edition of the Evening Post in New York City. *The ghostal arrangements which have for some time astonished the good people of Hydesville, Wayne County, and the surrounding neighborhood, continue still to be the wonder of the day. It seems that the mysterious rapping had been heard for a considerable length of time, at the great terror of the occupants of the house...The ghost was told that if he really was a spirit "to rap three times." The mysterious visitor complied, and the raps freezing the blood in the veins of the listeners. Other questions were asked and answered in the same way, the spirit informing his audience that it was murdered, and the body underneath the ground...The excitement now waxed high, and the crowds visited the haunted house."* Articles like the one in the Evening Post brought more people; they descended on the farm by the hundreds.

Between the crowds of spectators, and increased frequency and intensity of the strange phenomena, the girls' mother feared their safety. She sent them to live with their older sister Leah in Rochester. There, Kate and Maggie were embraced by the movers and shakers of society, including Amy and Isaac Post, Susan B Anthony and Horace Greeley. With their help, the sisters continued to showcase their abilities in parlors across the state and eventually Europe. Controversary followed them in the later years of their life, both having been accused of fraud. A headline in the Brooklyn Daily Eagle on March 9, 1893 announced "*Margaret Fox Kane, the Medium Dies,"* forty-five years to the month after their spiritual journey began. Kate died a year earlier. At the time of their deaths, both were penniless and broken in spirit.

Ten years after Kate and Maggie's death, an incredulous discovery was made in the old Hyde house which had sat empty for than half a century after the Fox family left. The story was carried in the November 24, 1904 edition of the New York Tribune, buried on page 10. Not newsworthy to most of the world, but important in corroborating the claims by the two young girls in 1848.

Can't Find Skull
Hunt for Bones in Home of Spiritualism Revives a Murder Story
Rochester, Nov. 23 - William H. Hyde, of the village of Hydesville, who recently found the arm and leg bones of a human

being in the house on his farm, in which modern spiritualism originated, this morning made another careful search of the cellar of the house. Mr. Hyde discovered all the other important bones of the body except the skull.

This corroborated the statement of Margaret Fox, which said that the spirit of a murdered man told her that his head had been severed from his body, placed in a stovepipe and thrown into the creek in front of the house. Mr. Hyde has securely fastened the openings to the house, and is waiting instruction from those high in spiritualism."

Could these be the mortal remains of the missing peddler, Charles Rosna? We will never know for certain.

In 1915 BF Bartlett bought the Hyde house and had it moved to the Spiritualist community of Lily Dale in Chautaugua County. A fire on September 21, 1955 destroyed the Fox sisters' childhood home, save the family Bible that had been storied in a small trunk. Divine intervention? All that remains of the original homestead on Hydesville Road is a crumbling old foundation. A memorial park has been built on the site, and the foundation is enclosed in a protective building as a sacred site of the Spiritualist Church.

THE PRESIDENT'S LAND

The town of Wayne in Steuben County has a small four rod square, or quarter acre, plot of land that belongs to the President of the United States. It was reported in the August 24, 1952 edition of the Democrat and Chronicle by Arch Merrill, a reporter who told the interesting stories of the history and people in Western New York.

There is a plot of land in the Town of Wayne, Steuben County, that belongs to the President of the United States. But I doubt if Harry Truman knows anything about it.

The deed to the Presidential holdings is recorded in the old stone office of the Steuben County Clerk in Bath. In that curious document, Moses Crookston, on Nov. 10, 1868, conveyed "to the President of the United States, because of the natural love and affection for my family, the property herein described, four rods square, in the Town of Wayne, reserving the right to burial for myself and wife and to be held as a burial place for my children."

The President in 1868 was Andrew Johnson. Moses Crookston was a prosperous farmer who had been a large wheat grower in the Civil War. The lot he deeded to the Chief Executive was part of his farm on the road that runs between Keuka and North Urbana, on a ridge high above Keuka Lake.

Crookston's motive is obscure. Perhaps he sought to insure perpetual care of his burial plot by deeding it to the President. If so, it was a grave error. Andrew Johnson and his successors have grossly neglected their property in the Town of Wayne.

Any recent President would have had a hard time even finding it. It was only through the help of Alderman Gleason that I located it...

He remembered the private cemetery on the Crookston land, said he has not seen it for years and volunteered to take me to it...

An 11-foot-high marble shaft on a stone base is surrounded by an ornate iron fence.

On the monument appear the names of "Moses Crookston who died Jan. 23, 1878, aged 72, and his wife, Sarah, who died Nov. 16, 1868, aged 70 years." On the obelisk is the epitaph:
> *Our parents –*
> *Our father and mother are gone*
> *They lay beneath the sod*
> *Dear parents, although we miss you much*
> *We know you rest with God*

Moses and Sarah Crookston married on August 7, 1819, and had ten children. He ran a large farm and a store on Keuka Lake. When Sarah died, Moses had this lovely tribute carved into the monument:
> *Shed not for me the bitter tears,*
> *Nor give thy heart to rain regrets:*
> *Tis but the casket that lies here,*
> *The gem that fills it sparkles yet.*

At the time of Merrill's article, the cemetery was overgrown and in deplorable condition. It had not always been like that. According to an interview with Moses' son at the turn of the 20th century, a "government man" came out to Wayne to visit and clean the cemetery, but the visits eventually stopped. In 1959 volunteers from the local grange clean it up. Today the cemetery is a proud moment of a man's love of family and country.

TROUTBURG

Near the end of the nineteenth century there were no fewer than twenty summer resorts along the shore of Lake Ontario from one end of Monroe County to the other. Some have familiar names - Summerville, Sea Breeze, Glen Haven, Newport and Crescent Beach to name a few. These were where the "summer people" flocked to.

One of the first simmer resorts, and one of the least known, began as a small fishing station at the very western edge of Monroe County in 1820. In fact, Troutburg straddled the boundary of Monroe and Orleans Counties at the end of present-day Route 272. The name was chosen to represent the large number of lake trout that were caught there. Hiram Redmond, who ran the fishing station, decided to open a "hotel" that provided entertainment for the fishermen. For decades it catered solely to men who fished, as it was surrounded by forests and farmland, offering none of the creature comforts that "gentler sex" was accustomed to.

Troutburg did not earn resort status until just prior to the outbreak of the American Civil War. In the late 1840s, Asa Lee bought a beautiful piece of land along the lake shore with grand plans to build on it. But those plans did not come to fruition, and it was left wild until 1860 when it was passed to his daughter-in-law Sarah. She began construction on a first-class resort which put Troutburg on the map. It became a destination point for people from miles around. Ms. Lee's property had a beautiful house, picnic grounds and a barn large enough to board as many as sixty horses at one time. There were two sailboats, and several rowboats docked at the pier for the guests to use. At first overnight accommodations were not available at the Lee House. This did not keep people away; they pitched tents in the grove. By 1874, guests could rent rooms in the house for a reasonable rate.

Soon there were three hotels in Troutburg, and none had any trouble being booked all summer long. When the summer heat bore down on the city of Rochester, the wealthy traveled out to the countryside to escape the heat and enjoy the refreshing lake breezes and swim in the cool waters.

The Ontario House was built by Silas Holbrook in the 1890s on the spot where the Lee House had once stood. In the book titled *The History of Brockport with Vicinity Happenings* by AB Elwell (1956), the author writes "After the building was displaced by the Ontario House..." There are no formal reports about what happened to the Lee House, though memoirs of those living in the area at the time allude to it being destroyed by fire. When Mr. Holbrook built the Ontario House, he only allowed six weeks for construction to be completed, which was a lofty deadline. Amazingly it was finished on time, and not only was there a beautiful hotel, but also a grand dance hall and a picnic pavilion.

William Bush built his hotel across the street from the Ontario House. Bush's property has a restaurant, bowling alley with a bar and picnic grounds. In *The History of Brockport with Vicinity Happenings,* one of the contributors remembers, "There was a hand operated merry-go-round on the front lawn on the Bush resort. A man would be sent out to turn the crank if enough riders were present to make it worthwhile."

The Ontario House

The Cady House was the third hotel at Troutburg, and it was by far the largest. The Cady House was part of Cady Groe, a large piece of land between William Bush's hotel and the lake. Cady

Grove had a dance hall as well as picnic grounds that were popular with Sunday school groups, churches and businesses. The Cady House burned down but would eventually be rebuilt. The family later added cottages which they rented out.

The harbor at Troutburg had several docks to accommodate ships from Canada loaded with lumber and other goods, as well as excursion steamers that took tourists to Coeburg, Ontario, Canada. In fact, the first ferry to cross Lake Ontario departed from Troutburg.

The resort was a fury of excitement. The Ontario Gun Club met south of Cady Grove for skeet shooting competitions. Boat racing was popular during the late 19th century, especially at the Brockport Yacht Club. Throughout the sailing season, several cup races were run along Lake Ontario's south shore, including the Gordon Cup. There was never a dull moment. The excitement did not just come from the resort hotels and grounds, sometimes the excitement was brought to them.

Until 1920 and before the passing of the Walker Law, prize fighting was illegal in New York state. This didn't stop the fights from happening, promoters just got creative with the venues. During the night Sunday August 23, 1885, the steamer *Angler* left the Port of Rochester, early the next morning the *Charlotte* followed suit. Both were filled with passengers who paid a hefty ticket price of $5 to go to Oak Orchard to watch Rochester's Patrick Slattery take on William Baker from Buffalo. When the steamers docked, there were no boxers or a ring to be found. Orleans County Sheriff Howard had arrested Slattery and Baker, holding them in Albion jail. By 10:30am on August 24, 1885, the judge has arraigned them and charged them with conspiracy to engage in a prize fright. They were released from jail but not before paying the $400 bond. Quickly Baker and Slattery got out of town with about two hundred men who had paid to see a fight. While the boxers were before the judge, their promoter scrambled to find a new location for the match. Hours later a ring sat in Cady Grove and bets were taken. At 4:48pm Slattery and Baker stepped into the ring as the referee read the Marquis de Queensbury rules. With a handshake the match began, and the men pummeled each other for six rounds. According to an article in the Rochester Democrat and Chronicle, "...their faces showed the effects of the brutal punishment." Baker put Slattery on the ropes, fouled and in a controversial decision Slattery was declared the winner. As fast as the ring went up, it came down. And before the police could show up with the paddy wagons, the crowd scattered. The fighters and their entourage hopped the Rome-Watertown train at the Morton station and hightailed it to Rochester.

Prize fighting was not the only illegal activity that took place at Troutburg. During Prohibition rum runners used the cloak of darkness to smuggle alcohol from Canada. The Rochester Democrat and Chronicle published an article in their July 7, 1924 edition about an arrest of some bootleggers caught near Troutburg. *"Six men from Rochester were arrested and being held at the Genesee County Jail in Batavia on the charge of transporting intoxicating liquor. Two thousand cases of Canadian ale and two trucks were confiscated right after the alcohol was unloaded from a boat that landed at Troutburg. The farm of Michael Cappizzi near Morton was the hiding place the bootleggers used. As for the boat and its captain, neither were caught. They had slipped into the darkness offshore and were long gone before the state police arrived."*

After the Great Depression hit the country, the hotels in Troutburg slowly closed their doors. William Bush sold his hotel to Edward Burns who turned it into his private summer home. Burns's friends Colonel Grief, who made his fortune in sugar, built a large summer estate on the west side of the county line. When Grief died, the Salvation Army bought the estate, and it became a summer camp for underprivileged children. The Ontario House burned down in 1943. A century of erosion at the foundation and shoreline, leaving the remnants about thirty feet out under the lapping waves. Of the fine hotels at Troutburg, the Cady House is the only one that remains standing, though it closed in 1941. Its windows long since broken by teenage vandals, decades of lake storms stripped the paint from its weathered boards, leaving an empty ghost of the past.

Troutburg is a ghost resort. The Storey House once familiar to many Rochesterians as a popular dining place, is only a heap of rubble. It burned down two years ago. The dance hall under the willows is being dismantled. Dingy streamers, once gay, hang down from the rafters. The high water has eaten away at the piers, grass covers the cement walks along the shore..." (The Ridge: Ontario's Blossom Country, Arch Merrill 1944)

William Bush's grandson said it best in his 1970s memoirs - "*To recall my childhood and youth in this prosperous little farming community and pleasant lakeside resort is an exquisite pleasure...Now, the bulwark of America, the family farm, has gone down the drain, and little hamlets of Troutburg and Morton are but pitiful derelicts of a wonderful past.*"

www.ingramcontent.com/pod-product-compliance
Lightning Source LLC
LaVergne TN
LVHW012026060526
838201LV00061B/4490